LEAVING CERTIF

LESS STRESS MORE SUCCESS

Music Revision
Higher Level

Vivienne Conway

GILL EDUCATION

Gill Education
Hume Avenue
Park West
Dublin 12
www.gilleducation.ie

Gill Education is an imprint of M.H. Gill & Co.

© Vivienne Conway 2022

ISBN 978 07171 94322
Design by Liz White Designs
Print origination by Sarah McCoy

For permission to reproduce photographs, the author and publisher
gratefully acknowledge the following:

© Alamy: 56, 96; © Frances Marshall: 41; © iStock/Getty Premium: 115;
© Jeff Hockberg/Getty Images: 129; © State Examinations Commission:
219, 220; © Wikimedia Commons: 3, 24, 70.

CONTENTS

Introduction...v

Section 1: The Listening Paper

1. Set Works 1

Set A

J. S. Bach, Cantata BWV 78: *Jesu, der du meine Seele* 3

Pyotr Ilyich Tchaikovsky, *Romeo and Juliet Fantasy Overture*.............. 24

Gerald Barry, *Piano Quartet No. 1* 41

Queen, *Bohemian Rhapsody*.. 56

Set B

Wolfgang Amadeus Mozart, *Piano Concerto No. 23
in A Major, K488* 70

Hector Berlioz, *Symphonie Fantastique Op. 14* 96

Raymond Deane, *Seachanges* (with Danse Macabre) 115

The Beatles, Songs from *Sgt. Pepper's Lonely Hearts Club Band* 129

2. Irish Music 147

Listening Section.. 147

Essay Section 152

3. Aural Skills...161

General Information.. 161

Preparing for the Examination 161

Musical Features and Techniques 163

The Exam.. 164

Aural Skills Key Words... 167

Section 2: Composition

4. Music Theory and Terminology...173

Pitch... 175

Note Values 177

Time Signatures 178

Key Signatures 179

Tempo... 180

Dynamics 181

Articulation 181

5. Melody 184

Question 1 184

Question 2 200

Question 3 200

6. Harmony...201

Chords.. 201

The Basics of Harmony 202

Question 5... 206

Question 4... 215

Section 3: Performance

7. The Practical Exam...219

Resources for the Practical Exam 219

Performing Skills.. 221

Music Technology 224

Unprepared Tests 228

Introduction

The Leaving Certificate Music exam is worth a total of 400 marks. These marks are divided into three core sections worth 25% or 100 marks each.

Section	Marks	Exam
Practical	100	Normally around Easter
Listening	100	June
Composition	100	June

The remaining 25% (100 marks) is an **elective**. This means that the candidate can choose to place these marks on to any of the above sections.

The elective allows the candidate to allocate a total of 50% of their overall marks to their strongest section of the Music course. Most candidates chose the performance elective, as they feel that is their strongest section.

Here is a breakdown of the full examination requirements:

Listening	Requirements
Core (100 marks)	● Four prescribed works ● Irish music ● Aural skills
Elective if chosen (100 marks)	*In addition to core exam* Study of a chosen special topic. This is completed after the core listening and composition core exams in June.

Composition	Requirements
Core (100 marks)	● Melody: Complete one of three questions ● Harmony: Complete one of three questions
Elective if chosen (100 marks)	*In addition to core exam* Presentation of a portfolio in one of the following ways: ● Present two short pieces and/or songs, composed, arranged, or orchestrated by the candidates *or* ● Present compositions and/or arrangements and/or orchestrations only (combined performance time approximately five minutes)

Practical	Requirements
Core (100 marks)	● Perform three songs or pieces ● One unprepared test
Elective if chosen (100 marks)	*In addition to core exam* ● Perform a programme of approximately 12 minutes' duration that reflects a further expansion of the Higher Level performing activity

Resources for the Leaving Certificate Music Exam

Website	Information provided
www.education.ie	● Leaving Certificate Music Syllabus ● Guidelines for teachers
www.examinations.ie	● Past exam papers and audio files ● Past unprepared tests ● Past marking schemes ● Information notes regarding exams ● Chief Music Examiner's reports
www.ppmta.ie	● Information regarding student and teacher workshops ● A vast amount of resources covering all areas of the curriculum

Approach to Study and Revision

Your approach to study and revision should reflect adequate time spent on **practical**, **composition** and **listening**. Let us look at the overall breakdown of marks for each question in each of the sections, assuming the candidate is taking the practical elective (50%).

Listening (100 marks)

Question	Subject	Marks
1	One of four set works	25
2, 3 and 4	Three of four set works	10 each
5	Irish Music	25
6	Aural Skills	20

Composition (100 marks)

Question	Subject	Marks
1, 2 or 3	Melody	40
4, 5 or 6	Harmony	60

Practical (200 marks)

Question	Content	Marks
Prepared work	Chosen songs/pieces	180
Unprepared work	Sight tests or aural memory or improvisation	20

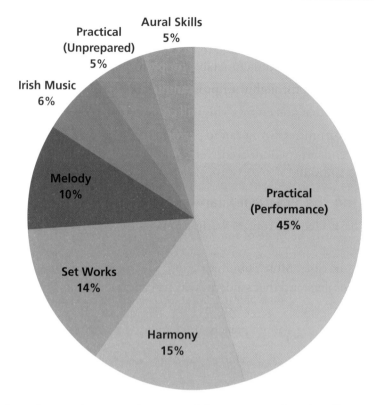

The pie chart shown gives an indication of the amount of marks allocated for each component in the entire exam.

The Practical Exam

The practical exam (including the unprepared test) carries the most amount of marks if it is your chosen elective (50% of the entire course).

Preparing for the Practical Exam

Be familiar with the requirements and seek out the information note on the practical exam that is issued to the school each year.

- Try out all of your performance options, including:
  - Sing/play with a group
  - Solo sing to your own accompaniment
  - Solo sing/play
  - Music technology
- Try out all of your unprepared test options, including:
  - Sight reading
  - Aural memory
  - Improvisation

- Seek advice from your Music teacher on what they think you may achieve the highest marks for.
- Make adequate time in your study timetable for performance practice.
- Ensure that you can play through your programme comfortably and confidently.
- Try to choose pieces that you enjoy – this will come across in the exam.
- Take as many opportunities as you can to perform in front of an audience: lunchtimes, class concerts, school events, etc. All of these experiences help you to build confidence and skill.

Before and During the Practical Exam

- Make sure you have adequate time to warm up and tune your instrument (if playing) before the exam.
- Relax and take your time. Most examiners are or have been classroom Music teachers, so they understand that students may feel a little nervous on the day. This is completely natural.
- Try to keep a flow to your chosen pieces/songs and don't panic if you make a small error in your performance.

The Composition Exam

For many students, the composition paper can be the most challenging on the course. It is important to assess your knowledge and build on it as you work through the Leaving Certificate Music course. Some students may have taken Music as a Junior Cycle subject, or take music lessons outside of school; therefore they enter the subject with a good level of knowledge of musical theory. Other students may begin Leaving Certificate Music with little or no experience of musical theory.

Preparing for the Composition Exam

- Go through past exam questions and be ready to handle any melody or harmony that could come up on the paper.
- Be familiar with the basics; keys (major and minor), notes values, chords, various time signatures, how to handle an anacrusis, etc.
- Time yourself when completing a composition task. Get ready to be able to complete both questions within the allotted time of 1 hour and 30 minutes. The melody is worth 40 marks and the harmony is worth 60 marks; therefore you may need to allocate more time to the harmony question.

Before and During the Composition Exam

- Make sure you have a strong pencil and rubber; you want your answers to be legible. Remember the examiner will be playing your work when they are marking.
- Use the rough work and jot down your variations in the melodies, chord boxes, staves, etc.

- Manage your time well. This should be practised before the exam, so you will go into the exam with a strategy on time: for example, 35 minutes on melody and 45 minutes on harmony.
- Check and re-check before finishing the exam. Make sure you have written in the correct key, include suffixes such as # or m, correct amount of beats in the bar, etc.

The Listening Exam

This part of the exam may involve the most amount of study for the student. There is a lot of information to absorb when it comes to the topics on the listening paper. However, this exam tests your ability to recognise and describe musical elements in what you **hear** in the exam.

Preparing for the Listening Exam

- Make sure you understand the basic key terms and phrases that are used throughout the listening section.
- Listen to your set works as often as possible.
- Make sure you are familiar with the sound of orchestral instruments.
- Plan your study sessions and set particular goals within a study session.
- Work through the exam papers and be familiar with the marking schemes.
- Keep a listening journal. Document all of the pieces of Irish music you listen to over the course of your study. This will come in useful when you are looking for musical examples for your Irish essay.

Before and During the Listening Exam

- Read the question carefully. Underline key words in the question. Are you being asked to reference the melody, accompaniment, or countermelody?
- Tick the correct amount of boxes in a multiple choice question. If you are asked for two answers, do not tick three or you may lose marks.
- Lay out your answers clearly and concisely. This is especially relevant when asked to compare and contrast two different sections of a work.
- Don't waste too much time on one particular question in an excerpt.
- If you have time at the end, use it to read through your answers.

1 Set Works

aims By the end of this chapter, you will be able to:
- have studied the prescribed set works
- know the musical features and understand the key words associated with each work
- be prepared to answer exam-style questions on each set work

exam focus

WORKS TO BE EXAMINED

SET B (2022)
- Wolfgang Amadeus Mozart, *Piano Concerto No. 23 in A Major, K488* (1786)
- Hector Berlioz, *Symphonie Fantastique Op. 14* (1830)
- Raymond Deane, *Seachanges* (with *Danse Macabre*) (1993)
- The Beatles, Songs from *Sgt. Pepper's Lonely Hearts Club Band* (1967)

SET A (2023–2025)
- J. S. Bach, Cantata BWV 78, *Jesu, der du meine Seele* (1724)
- Pyotr Ilych Tchaikovsky, *Romeo and Juliet Fantasy Overture* (1880)
- Gerald Barry, *Piano Quartet No. 1* (1992)
- Queen, *Bohemian Rhapsody* (1975)

Answering Questions on Set Works

Key words that are used in set works questions are:

- Identify
- Describe
- Explain
- Discuss

Identify is commonly a one word or short phrase answer and may be worth one or two marks. For example:

'Identify the section ...'

'Identify the instrument that plays ...'

'Identify the theme heard ...'

Describe and **explain** generally demand a more detailed answer. Both of these words regularly follow **identify** in a question. For example:

'Identify and describe the compositional technique heard ...'

'Identify and describe the instrumental technique heard on the violin ...'

Discuss is often used for questions that are worth more than one mark, and may demand that you show a more in-depth knowledge of the work. For example:

'Discuss how the composer portrays the spirit of the Danse Macabre in the work ...'

'Discuss the Mexican influences in ...'

Try to incorporate an example in your answer to this type of question. For example:

'Deane refers to the Mexican street musicians known as mariachi bands in this work. He does this by the use of the marimba, maracas and guiro. He also instructs the cello and violin to strum the strings, which alludes to the sound of the guitar in the mariachi band (Totentanz). All musicians play the maracas at the end of the work.'

Set Works A

J. S. Bach
Cantata BWV 78, *Jesu, der du meine Seele*

- A **cantata** is a musical work written for vocalists and instrumentalists. Historically, it has a liturgical setting and was part of the Lutheran church service. It usually has several movements such as a chorus, arias, recitatives and a **chorale**.

- A **chorale** is a German hymn tune written for four voices: soprano, alto, tenor and bass.

Johann Sebastian Bach was born in Germany in 1685. He is regarded as a key composer of the Baroque era and one of the most influential composers of all time. In 1724, Bach was assigned a post as director of church music in the city of Leipzig. There, part of his duties was to compose a cantata for the Sunday services. Bach wrote over 200 cantatas during his lifetime, and it is believed that at times he wrote one every week.

Bach's cantatas were usually written for a Baroque orchestra consisting of a string section, an oboe section and a **continuo** group.

A **continuo** group is common to Baroque music. It commonly consists of bass instruments such as cello and a keyboard instrument.

Background to *Jesu, der du meine Seele*

The cantata *Jesu, der du meine Seele* was written for the 14th Sunday after Trinity in the Lutheran liturgical calendar. The title translates as *'Jesus, by Thy Cross and Passion'*. The gospel for the 14th Sunday tells the story of the healing of the ten lepers. Throughout the cantata, Bach represents the emotional tone of this gospel story: sin, redemption, forgiveness and hope.

Key Words

Cantata	A musical work for voices with an instrumental accompaniment, usually with solos and chorus.
Chorale	A German hymn tune associated with the German Lutheran Church.
Chorus	A large, organised group of singers.
Aria	A song for a soloist with orchestral accompaniment, from an opera, oratorio or cantata.
Recitative	A style of singing whereby the singer(s) uses the rhythms and delivery of normal speech.
Recitative secco (Dry recitative)	A recitative with chordal accompaniment played by continuo.
Recitative accompagnato (Accompanied recitative)	A recitative with a more active accompaniment.
Chaconne	A musical work that contains a repetitive bass ostinato.
Figured bass	Number and figures written underneath a bass line that indicate chords.
Continuo	A single bass line played by cello and bass. The keyboard instrument also plays the bass line.
Violone	A four string bass instrument popular during the Baroque era. It precedes the double bass.
Appogiatura	A form of ornamentation that delays the next note of the melody, taking half of its written time value.
Melisma	Singing more than one note per syllable.
Syllabic	Singing one note per syllable.
Inversion	Turning a melody upside-down.
Antiphon	Where two groups of voices sing or play in imitation, one after the other. This is also known as call and response.
Parallel 3rds and 6ths	Where two voices separated by a third or sixth interval move in the same direction.
Da capo aria	A musical form in three sections (ABA) where the third section is a repeat of the first section.
Tierce de Picardie	A major third of the tonic heard at the end of a minor key piece.

Canon	Strict imitation between two or more parts at a fixed pitch and distance.
Pedal note	The bass note is held or sustained while the harmony changes. This is commonly used for effect or to transition from one key to another.

Instrumentation and Voices

Strings	Woodwind	Brass	Voices
Violin I	Flute	Horn	Soprano
Violin II	Oboe I		Alto
Viola	Oboe II		Tenor
Continuo (cello and harpsichord)			Bass
Violone			

Outline of Movements

Movement	Type	Voice	Key Signature	Time Signature
1	Chorus	SATB choir	G minor	3/4
2	Aria duet	Soprano and alto	B♭ major	Common
3	Recitative	Tenor	No key centre	Common
4	Aria	Tenor	G minor	6/8
5	Recitative	Bass	C minor and E♭ major	Common
6	Aria	Bass	C minor	Common
7	Chorale	SATB choir	G minor	Common

Texture and *Jesu, der du meine Seele*

Many parts of *Jesu, der du meine Seele* are polyphonic or contrapuntal.

Polyphonic or contrapuntal texture occurs when two or more independent melodies can be heard at the same time.

Polyphonic texture is a very popular feature of Baroque music.

In the exam, students are usually asked to identify and describe the texture of a given excerpt.

It is important to reference the music when asked about texture; describe which instruments are playing the melody or which voices are singing the melody.

Polyphonic texture occurs when a melody is heard in imitation by another voice or instrument.

Movement 7: Chorale

The chorale melody of Movement 7 is first heard in the opening movement of the cantata. It is important to understand the key features and terms associated with the chorale of Movement 7 before approaching Movement 1.

Soprano

FEATURES

- 16-bar melody
- Melody heard on soprano/violin I/flute/oboe I and horn
- Repeated notes in the melody

- AABC form
- Key and modulations: G minor – F major – B♭ major – G minor
- Altos, tenors and basses sing in harmony

- Cadence at the end of every two bars
- Last chord is G major
- Instruments double the vocal parts

Practise singing or playing the soprano line in the chorale. Parts of the chorale have appeared as a dictation question in past years.

It may be useful to use tonic solfa when singing through the chorale.

Movement 1: Chorus

Voices	Instruments	Form	Key Signature	Time Signature
SATB choir	Full orchestra	Ritornello	G minor	3/4

Movement 1 was written in the style of a **chaconne**. This was a very popular style of writing during the Baroque period. The composer uses a short harmonic progression that is then repeated many times during the piece. In this movement, Bach presents the **ostinato** or **descending theme** in several forms and keys throughout.

Ostinato/Descending Theme

FEATURES

- Octave leap
- Repeated notes
- Descending chromatic movement

- Mostly crotchet movement
- Ends with a perfect cadence
- G minor

Ritornello/Grief Theme

Ritornello form was a popular musical structure during the Baroque period. It is a work that contains a recurring or 'returning' section in between different episodes or musical passages.

In Movement 1, the ritornello theme is also known as the 'Grief' theme.

FEATURES

- Starts on second beat of the bar
- Dotted rhythm
- Leap of a sixth at the start
- Ends on a perfect cadence

Joy Motif

FEATURES

- Semiquaver and quaver movement
- Starts on the weak beat
- Rising sequence

Analysis of Movement 1: Chorus

The texture of most of this movement is polyphonic or contrapuntal. Be familiar with the themes and which instrument is playing them.

A variation on the chorale is heard in the soprano part. Although this work is in **ritornello form**, the movement can be studied with the AABC structure of the chorale in mind.

	Bar	Key	Melody	Countermelodies and Accompaniment	Points of Interest
A	1	G minor	**Ritornello** on flute, oboe I and violin I	**Ostinato theme** on continuo	Key of G minor Continuo = double bass, cello and harpsichord

Bar		Part 1	Part 2	Part 3
10		Ostinato theme on oboe I Countermelody on oboe II	Quaver movement on violins and viola (countermelody)	Polyphonic texture No continuo in bars 10–16
17		Ostinato theme in imitation on altos, tenors and basses	Joy motif in continuo Strings and oboe play accompaniment figure	Melisma in vocal parts
21		First half of phrase 1 of the chorale sung by sopranos and played by flutes Ritornello theme on violin I and oboe I	Ostinato theme on continuo	Dynamic marking *forte*
25		Inverted ostinato theme sung in imitation on altos and tenors Quaver melody on oboe I with countermelody on oboe II	Quaver movement on continuo	Polyphonic texture
29		Ostinato theme on bass with continuo	Quaver movement on oboe I	
33		Second half of phrase 1 of chorale on sopranos and flute Ritornello theme on violin I	Ostinato theme on continuo	Grief and ostinato theme continue at bar 37
41		Oboes and violins play in counterpoint	Violin II plays ostinato theme	Oboe and violins only
49		Vocal parts of bars 16–36 are repeated with different text	Joy theme on continuo	
69		Ostinato theme on violin I	Pedal note D major chord on continuo and vocals	Counterpoint between violins and oboe

A

	Bar	Key			
Link	73	D minor	**Inversion of ostinato** on tenors, altos and basses Busy semiquaver melody, then Grief motif on oboes in counterpoint	**Joy theme** on continuo **Ostinato theme** on violins	Modulation to D minor
	81	F major	First half of phrase 2 of the chorale on sopranos and flutes	Descending semiquavers in imitation on tenors then altos Ostinato theme on basses and continuo	V–I cadence in F major at bars 84–85
B	85		**Ritornello theme** on violin I, oboe I and flute	**Ostinato theme** on continuo	Short version of ritornello heard
	89		**New musical idea** in imitation on altos, tenors and basses	**Joy theme** on continuo	Musical idea based on a raised fourth note and repeated notes Voices enter one bar apart
	92	B♭ major	Second half of phrase 2 chorale sung by sopranos	**Ostinato theme** on continuo and basses **Joy motif** on violin I	Modulation to B♭ major
	99		**Ritornello theme** on violin I, oboe I and flute	**Ostinato theme** on continuo	Short ritornello in B♭ major
	103		**Musical idea from bar 89** heard with antiphony between flute and violin	**Joy theme** heard throughout between instrumental parts	**Antiphonal dialogue** between instruments in this section
C	107	G minor	**Ostinato theme** in imitation in tenor, alto, then bass	**Joy theme** in continuo, oboe and violin	Modulation to G minor
	118		First half of phrase 3 in soprano and flute	**Ritornello theme** on oboe and violin Ostinato theme in continuo	Short version of Grief theme
	121		**Joy theme** on violins	**Ostinato theme** in oboe and flute	Pedal note D on continuo

125		New motif played in antiphony in violins, flute and oboe	**Joy theme** in imitation on viola and continuo	Parallel thirds between violins I and II
129		Another new melodic motif in imitation between tenors, altos and basses	**Ritornello theme** motif on violins and oboes **Joy theme** on continuo and violas	Dynamic marking *piano*
137		**Second half of phrase 3** on sopranos and flute	**Ostinato theme** in continuo and basses	Dynamic marking *forte*
140		**Ritornello theme** on violins, flute and oboe	**Ostinato theme** on continuo	Ends on perfect cadence in G major (Tierce de Picardie)

exam focus

SAMPLE EXAM QUESTION

Compare and contrast the appearance of the chorale in Movement 1 and Movement 7.

Sample answer

- The chorale is set to 3/4 time in Movement 1 and common time in Movement 7.
- In Movement 7, each phrase lasts two bars. Each phrase is extended in Movement 1.
- The rhythm patterns of the chorale melody differs in Movement 1 and Movement 7.
- Both appearances of the chorale follow the same modulations.
- Both versions of the chorale end on a G major chord.
- Sopranos sing the chorale line in both movements.

Movement 2: Aria Duet

Voices	Instruments	Form	Key Signature	Time Signature
Soprano and alto	Violone continuo	Da capo aria	B♭ major	Common

This movement is contrapuntal in style, that is, many parts are polyphonic. The soprano and alto voices sing in imitation, which leads to melodies overlapping. There are also a lot of harmonies sung in parallel thirds and sixths.

Ritornello Theme

FEATURES

- B♭ major
- Rocking quaver movement
- Starts on an upbeat
- Ends on a perfect cadence

Vocal Theme

FEATURES

- Starts on an upbeat
- Melismatic setting
- Rising sequence
- Canon between soprano and alto voices

	Bar	Key	Melody	Accompaniment	Points of Interest
	1	B♭ major	**Ritornello theme** on continuo	Crotchet movement on violin	Ends on V–I cadence
A	8		Soprano introduces vocal theme followed by alto at bar 10 in canon at a fourth	Continuation of ritornello and violone Accompaniment throughout	Word-painting on 'eilen' Polyphonic texture Parallel sixths between soprano and alto at bars 14–15 Parallel thirds between soprano and alto at bar 19
	28		**Antiphonal dialogue** between soprano and alto on the words 'O Jesu, o meister'		Parallel sixths at bar 31 'eilen' Vocals end on a perfect cadence in B♭ major at bars 41–42

	Bar	Key		Description	Notes
	42		**Ritornello theme** on continuo		Ends on V–I cadence in B♭ major
	50	G minor	**Imitation** between soprano and altos		Key change to G minor Longer notes in melody line Perfect cadence in C minor at bar 60
	60	C minor	**Ritornello theme** on continuo in C minor		No vocals
B	64	G minor D minor F major	Soprano and alto sing in parallel thirds '*Ach! Höre*' Imitation in parts between alto and soprano		Modulation to G minor Perfect cadence in D minor at bar 80 Short ritornello in F major at bar 80
	83	F major	Imitation between alto and soprano		Modulation to F major Parallel thirds and melisma on the word '*erfreulich*' at bars 88 and 89 Section ends on a perfect cadence in F major
A	1		Return to A		

Word-painting in Movement 2: Aria Duet

Bar	Word	Word-painting
9	'*eilen*' (hurry)	**Melisma:** sung with ascending quavers and semiquavers, portraying a sense of anticipation
28	'*O Jesu, O Meister*' (Oh Jesus, Oh Master)	**Repetition of words:** emphasises the importance of words
96	'*erfreulich*' (cheerful)	**Melisma:** sung with ascending quavers and semiquavers, portraying a sense of happiness

Word-painting is a popular question in this set work. Be familiar with examples of word-painting in the relevant movements.

Movement 3: Tenor Recitative

Voices	Instruments	Key Signature	Time Signature
Tenor	Continuo	No key centre	Common

This movement is a recitative *secco*. This usually has very sparse accompaniment.

There is no key centre.

It is sung in a declamatory style, therefore it is more like a dramatic speech than a melody.

The word setting is syllabic.

The melody contains wide leaps and diminished intervals that enhances the importance of certain words and phrases.

The harmony contains diminished and seventh chords, which emphasises the dramatic nature of the text.

Bar	Points of interest
1	Dynamic marking **piano** on continuo Ambiguity in key centre Melody opens with an interval of an **augmented fourth**
6	Tenth **leap** in the tenor line
20	More melodic tenor line and more movement in continuo
22	**Melisma** on the word *'erzürnet'* (anger)
24	Ends on a perfect cadence in **C minor**

Movement 4: Tenor Aria

Voices	Instruments	Form	Key Signature	Time Signature
Tenor	Traverse flute continuo	ABB' Dal segno	G minor	6/8

Dal segno means 'return to the sign'.

Ritornello Theme: Flute Obbligato

An obbligato in Baroque music refers to a musical part (the flute part in this case) that is essential to the piece.

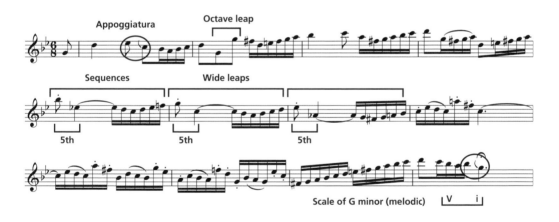

Scale of G minor (melodic) V   i

FEATURES

- Begins on an upbeat
- Sequences
- Semiquaver movement
- Rising scale
- Octave leaps
- Appoggiatura
- Syncopated rhythm
- Downward fifth leaps

	Bar	Key	Melody	Accompaniment	Points of Interest
A	1	G minor	**Ritornello theme** on the flute	Quaver movement in continuo	Ends on V–I cadence in G minor
					Homophonic texture
	12		Tenor sings a short phrase derived from the **ritornello theme** which is continued by the flute	Octave leaps	Mix of *legato* and *staccato* notes on the flute
				Cello plays *pizzicato*	
	18	B♭ major	Tenor sings with some parallel sixths on the flute		Music modulates to B♭ major
					Countermelody on the flute
					Polyphonic texture
	27		**Ritornello theme** shortened		Key of B♭ major
B	31	C minor	Tenor melody with flute countermelody		Octave leaps on the words *'zum streite'* (assail me)
		E♭ major			Descending sequences on the flute
					Modulates to C minor
					Melisma on the word *'streite'* at bars 35–36
					Pedal note G in octaves on cello
					Perfect cadence in E♭ major at bar 42
	43	C minor	Short **ritornello** on flute in C minor		Tied notes on continuo
	45	G minor	Tenor and flute in counterpoint in G minor		Similar melody to B section
		C minor			Key changes from G minor to C minor and returns to G minor
		G minor			Dominant pedal note on the word *'stehet'* (stand) at bars 53–56
					Section ends with a perfect cadence in G minor
A	1		Dal segno: return to bars 1–12		

Many parts of the tenor aria are contrapuntal. If the exam question asks to describe texture, be sure to reference the two melodies: the tenor melody and the flute countermelody, played at the same time.

Word-painting in Movement 4: Tenor Aria

Bar	Word	Word-painting
32	'zum streite' (assail me)	Octave leaps used to emphasise the words
39	'beherzt' (support)	Word is repeated using rising sequences
51	'streite' (fight)	Melisma
53	'stehet' (stand)	Dominant pedal note to represent 'stand'

Movement 5: Bass Recitative

Voices	Instruments	Key Signature	Time Signature
Bass	Violins, viola continuo	E♭ major Ends in F minor	Common

This movement is a **recitative** *accompagnato*. The accompaniment is fuller than that in Movement 3, with the violins and viola accompanying as well as the continuo.

Changes in key, dynamics and texture alter the mood throughout.

There are three tempo changes that enhance the change in mood: *vivace* (very quick), *adagio* (slow) and *andante* (moderately slow).

The music moves through a number of key centres:

- Perfect cadence in **E♭ major** in bar 7
- Move to **G minor** in *vivace* section
- *Adagio* section ends in **E♭ major**
- *Andante* section moves to **F minor**

Although it is sung in a declamatory style, **the melody is more lyrical than that of Movement 3**. This is known as **arioso style** (like an aria).

The word setting is **syllabic**, with melisma on the words '*vermenget*' and '*besprenget*'.

The melody contains wide leaps and diminished intervals that enhance the importance of words and phrases.

The harmony contains diminished and seventh chords that emphasise the dramatic nature of the text.

The texture is **homophonic**.

Analysis of Movement 5: Bass Recitative

Bar	Points of interest
1	E♭7 chord at the start of bar 1
	Perfect cadence in E♭ major at bar 7
	Dynamic marking *piano*
	Sustained chords on strings
	Opening melody contains a seventh leap
	Wide descending leap '*Kron und Grab*'
	Syllabic style singing
8	Change of tempo to *vivace*
Vivace	Dynamic marking *forte*
	Key change to G minor
	Tempo change used to highlight the importance of the words
10	Tempo change to *adagio* in instruments and lento in bass voice
Adagio	Change of dynamics to *piano*
	Diminished and augmented harmonies
	Pedal note E♭ on continuo at bars 13–14
17	Most melodic section of the recitative
Andante	Some trills on bass line
	Strings play a more decorated accompaniment
	Vocals come to a close on a V–VI cadence in F minor
	Ends on a perfect cadence in F minor

Movement 6: Bass Aria

Voices	Instruments	Form	Key Signature	Time Signature
Bass	Oboe I	ABB'	C minor	Common
	Violins I and II	Dal segno		
	Viola			
	Continuo			

Ritornello Theme: Oboe and Violin I

FEATURES

- Starts on an upbeat
- Trills
- Dotted rhythm
- Ends with a perfect cadence

Oboe Solo

The ritornello theme is accompanied by a florid oboe solo.

FEATURES

- Semiquaver movement
- Scale passages
- Sequences

The key signature of this movement includes two ♭s, suggesting it is in the key of G minor. It is, however, actually in the key of C minor. Note the A♭s in the score.

Analysis of Movement 6: Bass Aria

Bar	Key	Melody	Points of Interest
Upbeat to 1	G minor	**Ritornello theme** on oboe and violin I with oboe semiquaver melody	Ends on V–I cadence in G minor Homophonic texture Mostly quaver movement in the continuo
Upbeat to 9		Bass sings a short phrase derived from the **ritornello theme** and is continued by the oboe	Polyphonic texture at bar 10 where the oboe and bass are heard at same time Melisma on word *'Rauben'*
12	C minor	**Ritornello** on strings followed by oboe solo	Key of C minor

A

	Bar	Key	Description	Notes
A	Upbeat to 17		Bass melody with oboe melody	Note the motif ♪♪♪ on the strings Wide leaps in bass
	20		Short ritornello heard along with bass melody in E♭ major	Oboe continues solo Melisma on the word 'Hoffnung' at bars 22–23
	Upbeat to 25	G minor	**Ritornello** in G minor followed by oboe solo	Perfect cadence in G minor at bar 32
B	Upbeat to 33	B♭ major	Bass melody moves to B♭ major **Ritornello** in F minor at bar 36	Pedal note C in the bass at bars 37–38 on the word 'Ewigkeit' Melisma on the word 'rauben' at bars 39–40
A'	Upbeat to 43	C minor	**Ritornello** in C minor followed by repeated text from section B	Bass melody is similar to melody at bars 9–10 Motif ♪♪♪ returns on strings at bar 46 Pedal note G in the bass at bars 49–50 on the word 'Ewigkeit'
	52		Decorated ending on the word 'rauben'	Perfect cadence in C minor
Dal segno	1		**Ritornello** and oboe solo at bars 1–8 to finish	Dal segno

Word-painting in Movement 6: Bass Aria

Bar	Word	Word-painting
11	'Rache' (troubled)	**Melisma:** sung over a number of semiquavers
22	'Hoffnung' (comfort)	**Melisma:** sung over a number of semiquavers
37	'Ewigkeit' (forever)	**Pedal note:** sustained note over a changing harmony
39	'Rauben' (protection)	**Melisma:** sung over a number of semiquavers

SAMPLE EXAM QUESTION

Describe how Bach presents the ritornello theme in Movement 6.

Sample answer

- The ritornello is first heard in the opening bars in the key of C minor. It is played by the oboe and violin I with string and continuo accompaniment.
- It is followed by the oboe solo melody.
- It is heard as an instrumental section and with the bass vocal.
- It is present in a number of keys such as B♭ major and G minor.
- The opening ritornello theme is heard again at the closing of the movement.

SAMPLE EXAM QUESTION

Identify two similarities and two differences between Movement 3 and Movement 5.

Sample answer

	Movement 3	Movement 5
Similarities	1. Wide leaps in the vocal line 2. Mostly syllabic word setting	
Differences	1. Tenor voice 2. No key centre until the end of the movement (C minor)	1. Bass voice 2. Key centres of E♭ major and F minor

Be sure to refer to both movements and clearly describe how they are similar and how they differ. It is not sufficient to simply describe one movement when asked to explain the differences.

Past Exam Questions

Year	Movement	Questions	Marks
2019 Q3 (6 marks)	3: Tenor Recitative	(a) The type of voice heard in this excerpt is: (multiple choice).	2
		(b) Identify two features of the vocal line heard in the excerpt.	2
		(c) There is a change of tempo mid-way through this excerpt. Describe one other change that takes place in the music from that point on.	2
2018 Q4 (10 marks)	5: Bass Recitative	*Excerpt 1* (i) Identify the type of voice heard in this excerpt.	1
		(ii) Identify two features of the vocal line heard in this excerpt.	3
		(iii) Identify one feature of the accompaniment heard in this excerpt.	1
		(iv) Identify the cadence heard at the end of this excerpt.	1
		(v) This excerpt is taken from: (multiple choice). Give a reason for your choice.	1+1
		Excerpt 2 (vi) The music in this excerpt is more dramatic than the music in excerpt 1. Explain why this is so and how it is achieved.	2
2017 Q3 (10 marks)	2: Aria Duet	(i) Name the movement from which this excerpt is taken. It is sung by: (multiple choice). The opening bars are sung in: (multiple choice).	1 1 1
		(ii) Identify two features of the vocal line in this excerpt: (multiple choice).	1

		(iii) Name the keyboard instrument that plays in this excerpt.	0.5
		The keyboard player reads from a figure bass. Explain.	1.5
		(iv) Identify the cadence heard at the end of this excerpt.	2
		(v) Describe one example of word-painting in your answer.	2

exam TIPS

- 'Identify the feature of the vocal music' may suggest an answer such as: 'The composer uses melisma/wide leaps/repeated notes/grace notes/chromatic movement in the vocal line. For example, on the word *"efreulich"* ...'

- Students are regularly asked to 'identify the cadence heard at the end of the excerpt'. Listen out for a finished or unfinished phrase. Use the terms **perfect, imperfect, plagal** or **interrupted** in your answer.

- Word-painting is a common feature in Bach's *Jesu, der du meine Seele*. Be aware of what the composer uses to emphasise a word or phrase. It is a good idea to make notes on examples of word-painting in each movement.

- Be familiar with features of Baroque style heard in this work.

Pyotr Ilyich Tchaikovsky
Romeo and Juliet Fantasy Overture

Pyotr Ilyich Tchaikovsky was born in Votkinsk, Russia, in 1840. He wrote a number of symphonies, ballets, suites and overtures and is regarded as the most popular Russian composer of his era. His is known for his beautiful and emotive melodies and orchestrations.

Tchaikovsky completed *Romeo and Juliet Fantasy Overture* in 1880. It was inspired by William Shakespeare's tragedy *Romeo and Juliet*, and is one of his best known works. It epitomises music from the Romantic era. The *Fantasy Overture* is an example of **programme music**, which is music that depicts a story or a mood. This style of writing music was hugely popular in Europe in the middle of the 19th century. In this work, Tchaikovsky takes three images from Shakespeare's play *Romeo and Juliet* and uses the orchestra to portray emotions: the theme of strife, representing the two feuding families (the Montagues and the Capulets) the theme of love; and the character of Friar Laurence.

> *Romeo and Juliet* is a **concert overture** – a one-movement orchestral work performed in a concert hall.

Features of Romantic Music in *Romeo and Juliet Fantasy Overture*

- Use of a large orchestra with an extensive use of brass and percussion
- Programme music is a feature of the Romantic era
- Expressive, dramatic emotive music made effective by the large orchestra and rich timbres
- Unusual instrumentation, e.g. the cor anglais and viola play the melody line for the love theme
- Extreme contrasts in dynamics
- Modulating to unrelated keys, e.g. B minor to D♭ major
- Rich harmonies

Key Words

Tempo Markings

Andante non tanto quasi moderato	Not too slow, almost moderate speed
Poco a poco string(endo)/accel(erando)	Getting faster little by little
String(endo) al ...	Getting faster to ...
Allegro guisto	Lively and steady
Moderato assai	Quite moderate

Instrumental Techniques and Expression Markings

Poco piu f	A little louder
Dolce	Sweetly
Mar./marcato	Well marked/accented
Dolce ma sensibile	Sweetly but sensitively
Legato	Smoothly
Pizz./pizzicato	Pluck the string
Con sordino	With a mute
Senza sordino	Without a mute
Div.	Divided
Unis.	Unison
Poco a poco cresc.	Getting gradually louder
Sempre	Always
Amoroso	Emotionally and tenderly
ppp	As soft as possible
fff	As loud as possible
Molto meno mosso	A lot less movement
a2	Two instruments play the same line of music

Revising the Basics

Revision for Tchaikovsky involves a partnership of listening and learning. Study the work under the headings listed below.

FEATURES

- Texture
- Compositional techniques
- Cadence points
- Terms and features associated with Romantic music
- Form
- Use of the harp as a link back to the intro

- Main key centres
- Main themes
- Use of dynamics and tempo
- Identification of themes in different sections
- Antiphonal dialogue between different sections of the orchestra

- Orchestration
- Instrumental techniques
- Rhythmic features
- Development of themes throughout the work
- Dynamic changes
- Modulations

Orchestra

Strings	Woodwind	Brass	Voices
Violin I	Piccolo	Horn (in F) ×4	Timpani (in E)
Violin II	Flute ×2	Trumpet (in E) ×2	Timpani (in B)
Violas	Oboe ×2	Tenor trombone ×2	Timpani (in F#)
Cellos	Clarinet (in A) I	Bass trombone ×2	Cymbals
Double basses	Clarinet (in A) II	Tuba	Bass drum
Harp	Cor anglais		
	Bassoon ×2		

Form

This work is in **sonata form**. Sonata form is a large-scale ABA form. In the Romantic era, composers developed the introduction and codas in a work in sonata form. The introduction to Tchaikovsky's *Romeo and Juliet Fantasy Overture* is over six minutes long and contains one of the main themes: the Friar Laurence theme.

Intro	Exposition (A)	Development (B)	Recapitulation (A)	Coda
Opening key of F♯ minor	Subject I (strife) in B minor	Variation on previously heard material	Return of Subjects I and II in B minor and D♭ major	Ending
Friar Laurence theme	Transition/link section	Various key changes		Subject II is prominent
Approximately six minutes long	Subject II (love) in D♭ major			Ends on B major chords
	Codetta			

The exposition in a sonata usually has two main themes. These themes are often referred to as Subjects I and II.

There are three main themes in this work: the first theme in the introduction, and the second and third themes (Subjects I and II) in the exposition section.

Common Musical Features Found in *Romeo and Juliet Fantasy Overture*

Melodic	Rhythmic	Compositional
Step movement	Dotted rhythm	Four-part harmony
Chromatic movement	Syncopation	Canon
Wide leaps	Tied notes	Sequences
Scalia movement	Semiquaver movement	Antiphony
Repeated notes	Crotchet and minim movement	Modulations

exam TIPS

The story of Shakespeare's *Romeo and Juliet* is told through the music of this fantasy overture. A common exam question is to identify and describe the use of programme music in this work. Tchaikovsky uses **three main themes** to present the characters and the drama of the plot.

Themes

The three main themes that are heard throughout *Romeo and Juliet Fantasy Overture* are:

- Friar Laurence
- Strife
- Love

Friar Laurence

This theme is first heard in the introduction to the work. It is also heard in the development and recapitulation section and is echoed in the chorale-like melody in the coda.

Here is the **Friar Laurence** theme in its original form.

FEATURES OF THE FRIAR LAURENCE THEME

- Mostly minim and crochet movement
- Mostly step movement
- Key of F# minor
- Chorale style with harmony in clarinet II and bassoons
- Melody played on clarinet I
- Sombre or solemn mood
- Ends on the chord of V
- Use of rests

PROGRAMME MUSIC

Friar Laurence is a religious character in the play. The music used at the very start of the work is in the style of a chorale – a German hymn tune, popular in the 17th century. The solemn nature of the key and tempo, along with the mellow woodwind instrumentation represent the character of Friar Laurence and a foreboding sense of tragedy and drama.

Strife (Subject I)

The **strife** theme is first heard in the opening section of the exposition. It is part of Subject I.

FEATURES OF THE STRIFE THEME

- Key of B minor
- Syncopated rhythm
- Dotted rhythm

- Semiquaver rhythm
- Four-bar melody
- Range of six notes

There are three short motifs within this theme.

1. Ascending and descending scale passages:

2. Semitone motif in sequence:

3. Answer and call (antiphony) between strings and woodwind family. This motif has a repeated rhythmic figure:

PROGRAMME MUSIC

The strife theme represents the tensions and conflict between the two families (the Montagues and the Capulets) in the play. A minor tonality, syncopated and dotted rhythm, along with rushing scales and a full orchestration portray this mood of tension and drama. The composer also uses percussion to add to this mood.

Love (Subject IIa and Subject IIb)

There are two parts to the love theme: Subject IIa and Subject IIb. This theme is first heard in the exposition. It is also heard in the recapitulation and coda sections.

FEATURES OF THE LOVE THEME

Subject IIa

- Key of D♭ major
- Played on viola and cor anglais
- Leaps of fourths and sixths
- Slow tempo
- Mellow tone
- Some step movement

Subject IIb

- Melody moves in crochets
- Strings play with mute
- Diminished fifths in melody
- Falling seconds in melody

PROGRAMME MUSIC

The love theme is in D♭ major. This key change from B minor takes the listener completely away from the tension and drama of the previous section of the work. The music in this section represents the gentle and romantic nature of the love between the two main characters. Tchaikovsky uses a light texture and mellow instruments such as the cor anglais and viola to express this mood.

Make sure you are fully aware of all features of the themes in their original forms. It is easier to understand variations on the themes when you have a full grasp on the original theme. A possible question may be to describe another section in the work (not heard in the exam) where the theme is heard. This is a possible three marks in a 10-mark question.

Analysis of the *Romeo and Juliet Fantasy Overture*

Introduction

Bar	Key	Subject/link	Accompaniment	Points of Interest
1	F# minor	**Friar Laurence** played on clarinet I	Clarinet II and bassoons ×2	Homophonic texture Solemn mood Chorale-like melody
11	Move to F minor	**Link (1)** Melody derived from opening bars Played on strings then woodwind	Pedal notes on double basses Cello plays crochets descending in thirds	Ascending F minor chords on harp Augmented second in flute Subtle changes in dynamics
39				Descending pizzicato strings
41	F minor	**Friar Laurence (2)** played on flute and oboe	Pizzicato strings play descending pattern Clarinets and bassoons	Theme played two octaves higher
52	Move to E minor	**Link (2)** Repetition on Link (1), played one semitone lower	See **Link (1)**	Augmented seconds in strings Link ends with a timpani roll and descending low strings
86	E minor	**Friar Laurence (3)** Played in **antiphony** between woodwind, horn and violas	Pedal note in double basses Short notes on strings Timpani rolls	Change in tempo (*allegro*) Loud dynamics Chromatic variation of Friar Laurence theme
105		End of introduction		Antiphony between woodwind and strings on chord of B minor

Exposition: Subject I

Bar	Key	Subject/link	Accompaniment	Points of Interest
112	B minor	**Subject I (strife)** Played on flute and violin I	Woodwind, strings, horn	Loud dynamics Dotted rhythm Homophonic texture
115	B minor	**Subject I** **Ascending and descending scale motif** on strings		
118	B minor	**Subject I** **Semitone motif** played on woodwind, horns and violin II	Woodwind, strings, horn, timpani	Violin I plays repeated semiquavers
122	B minor	**Subject I** **Antiphony** between violin I and woodwind	Syncopated chords in horn and strings	Rhythmic motif taken from strife theme
126	D minor	**Subject I (strife) (2)** Played in canon between low strings and woodwind	Semiquavers on violins	Polyphonic texture
135		**Antiphonal dialogue** between violin I and woodwind		Dramatic build up
143	B minor	Semiquaver scale passages on strings	Syncopated chords on woodwind, brass and percussion	Cymbal and bass drum heard
151		**Subject I (strife) (3)** **Scale motif and semitone motif**	Full orchestra	Extra percussion Subject I ends with semiquaver scales and syncopated chords

Exposition: Transition and Subject II

The love theme can be heard three times in this section.

Bar	Key	Subject/link	Accompaniment	Points of Interest
164		Transition based on semiquaver motif	Pedal A in double basses Texture gets lighter as the music progress	Melody shifts from flute to clarinet, to bassoon, to double basses
184	D♭ major	**Subject IIa (love) (1)** Played by viola and cor anglais	Pizzicato cellos and double basses Syncopated chords on horns in F	Mute used on viola Ends with a D♭ major ascending broken chord on the harp
193		**Subject IIb (love) (1)** Played by violin I	Strings moving in crochets	Mutes used and string parts divided Crescendo with long notes on bassoon
213	D♭ major	**Subject IIa (love) (2)** Played by flute and oboe	Falling second motif played on horn Broken chords in quavers on strings	Theme is re-introduced by scale on flute and oboe
221		Lyrical melody on strings	Countermelody on horn Rocking quavers on strings A♭ pedal note on bassoon	Swelling dynamics Music is highly emotive Full texture
235	D♭ major	**Subject IIa (love) (3)** Played on flute and oboe	Similar to Subject IIa (2)	

243		**Ending of exposition**	Chords on harp	Pizzicato on cellos and double basses
		Melody alternates between bassoon and cor anglais	Long, sustained notes on strings	Echoes of music from the introduction
				Ends on viola playing an F

Development

Bar	Key	Subject/link	Accompaniment	Points of Interest
273	B minor	Hint of **strife theme** in strings		
280	F# minor	**Friar Laurence (4)** played on horns Inversion of **strife** in violin II	Semiquaver scales in strings	Polyphonic texture Syncopated repeated notes in strings Antiphonal dialogue between woodwind and brass
302	G minor	**Friar Laurence (5)** and inversion of **strife** repeated from previous section, but played one semitone higher		
315	Various keys	Fragments of **Friar Laurence** heard in woodwind Fragments of **strife** on strings		Full texture Build up in dynamics Dramatic mood
335	B minor and B major	**Friar Laurence (6 and 7)** played on trumpet in E	Full orchestra	Use of percussion
345	B minor	Semiquaver passage on strings	Syncopated chords in woodwind, brass and percussion	Development ends with a dramatic F# major chord

Instrumentation is commonly examined, so be familiar with the use of the orchestra. This applies to both the instruments playing the melody and the instruments in the accompaniment.

Recapitulation

Bar	Key	Subject/link	Accompaniment	Points of Interest
353	B minor	**Subject I (strife)** (4) **Scale motif, semitone motif**	**Full orchestra**	Dynamic marking *ff* Full texture Use of percussion Descending scale on strings at 365
368	D major	**Subject IIb (love)** (2) Played by oboes	Woodwind and swirling semiquavers in strings	Played sweetly and expressively; contrast from previous music Dramatic crescendo Triplet scale on strings at 388
389	D major	**Subject IIa (love)** (4) Played by strings and piccolo	Triplet quavers in woodwind Falling second motif on horns Descending bass	Pedal notes in bass at 396 Dramatic crescendo from 396 (material from exposition but fuller texture)
420	Changing keys	Fragments of **Subject IIa** played in imitation by cello, flute and bassoon	Strings playing repeated note triplet rhythm (hint of **strife**)	Dynamic changes Sense of panic in music Use of timpani at 434
436		**Subject IIa (5)** for five bars Played by strings	Syncopated chords on horn Full orchestra	Imitation between strings and woodwind Dynamics *ff* to *mf*
441		Fragments of **Subject I** and **Subject IIa**	Full orchestra	Intensity marked by bass drum and cymbals

446	B minor	**Subject I (5)** violin I and woodwind	Full orchestra *ff*	Percussion
450	Changing keys	**Friar Laurence (8 and 9)** woodwind and brass **Subject I (6)** on strings and woodwind	Full orchestra Abundant use of semiquaver motif and falling second motif	Alternating Friar Laurence with strife theme Changing keys Building intensity Climactic point at 473 *fff* Lighter texture towards end
481		**Final 4 bars** on bassoon, cellos and double basses		Last note F♯ with a timpani roll

Coda

Bar	Key	Subject/link	Accompaniment	Points of Interest
485	B major	Fragments of **Subject IIa**	Timpani roll Tonic pedal note on double basses and tuba	Triplet rhythm on timpani Pizzicato on double basses
495		Chorale-like melody on woodwind		Chorale melody and harp ascending chords recall the introduction
510		**Subject IIa** echoed on strings	Syncopated chords in woodwind Ascending chords on harp	
519		*ff* B major chords ends the overture		Chords played by full orchestra

SAMPLE EXAM QUESTION

Excerpt 1 = First appearance of Friar Laurence theme
Excerpt 2 = Second appearance of Friar Laurence theme

Identify similarities and differences in the music of excerpt 1 and 2.

Sample Answer:

Excerpt 1	Excerpt 2	Similarity/Difference
Friar Laurence theme	Friar Laurence theme	Similarity
Ends on chord V	Ends on chord V	Similarity
Key of F# minor	Key of F minor	Difference
Melody on clarinet in A	Melody on flutes and oboes	Difference
Accompaniment on clarinet II in A and bassoons	Accompaniment on pizzicato strings	Difference

Clearly outline your answer. You might like to draw a line down the centre of the answer space and outline the information under two headings, as above.

Past Exam Questions

Year	Movement	Questions	Marks
2019 Q1 (25 marks)	Excerpt 1: Recapitulation, Subject IIa	(a) Name two different instruments which play the melody in bars 1–8 of this excerpt.	2+2
		(b) Describe two features of the accompaniment in this excerpt.	2+2
	Excerpt 2: Bar 441, Subject IIa	(c) Describe the texture of the music heard in this excerpt.	3
	Excerpt 3: Recapitulation, Subject Ia	(d) Insert the five missing notes in bars 1 and 2, at **X** on the score.	3.5
		(e) Identify one feature which creates a feeling of conflict in the music heard in this excerpt.	1.5
	Excerpt 4: Coda, Subject IIa	(f) Name the section from which this excerpt is taken.	2
		(g) Name the theme on which this melody is based.	1
		(h) Describe two ways in which the thematic material heard in this excerpt differs from the first time it is heard in *Romeo and Juliet Fantasy Overture* by Tchaikovsky. You must refer to both sections in your answer.	2+2
	Excerpt 5: Coda, chorale-like section	(i) The music in this excerpt is often described as being like a chorale. Give one reason to support this statement with reference to the music heard in this excerpt.	2
2018 Q1 (25 marks)	Excerpt 1: Development, Friar Laurence (1)	(i) The melody heard at the start of this excerpt is based on the: (multiple choice).	1
		(ii) This excerpt is taken from the: (multiple choice).	2

		(iii) The music in this excerpt features antiphonal dialogue. Explain antiphonal dialogue, with reference to the music heard in this excerpt.	1+2
		(iv) The first two bars of the melody are printed below. Insert the four missing notes in bars 3 and 4, marked **X** on the score.	2+2
	Excerpt 2: Development, bar 335, Friar Laurence theme	(i) Describe two differences between the music heard in this excerpt and the music heard in excerpt 1. Refer to both excerpts in your answer.	3+3
	Excerpt 3: Start of Recapitulation	(i) The opening melody is played by: (multiple choice).	1
		(ii) The tonality of the music in this excerpt is: (multiple choice).	1
		(iii) Identify two features of the music heard in this excerpt.	1+1
	Excerpt 4: Recapitulation bar 368, Subject IIb	(i) Which one of the following rhythms can be heard quietly in the background?	1
		(ii) Describe two features of the music which immediately follows the music in this excerpt in *Romeo and Juliet Fantasy Overture*.	2+2
2017 Q4 (10 marks)	Excerpt 1: Opening of Exposition	(i) This excerpt is taken from the: (multiple choice).	1
		(ii) The theme heard in this excerpt is the: (multiple choice). Identify two features of this theme.	1 / 1+1
		(iii) This excerpt features dialogue between strings and woodwind. This dialogue is based on: (multiple choice).	1
		(iv) Describe Tchaikovsky's use of canon in the second half of this excerpt.	2
		(v) Describe two differences between the theme heard in this excerpt and one other theme from *Romeo and Juliet Fantasy Overture*.	1.5+1.5

2013 Q1 (25 marks)	Excerpt 1: Opening of Coda (bar 485)	(i) From which section of the work is this excerpt taken?	1
		(ii) Name the percussion instrument playing in this excerpt. It plays: (multiple choice).	1 1
		(iii) Name two instruments which play the melody in this excerpt.	1.5+1.5
		(iv) Describe the music played by the double bass in this excerpt.	2
	Excerpt 2: Bar 495, chorale- like section	(i) Insert the four missing melody notes at **X** on the score.	4
		(ii) Describe two ways in which the music of this excerpt differs from the music of excerpt 1.	2+2
		(iii) The texture of the music heard in this excerpt is: (multiple choice).	1
	Excerpt 3: Bar 510, Subject IIa	(i) Name the theme heard in bars 1–9 of this excerpt.	1
		(ii) Describe one feature of the accompaniment in bars 1–9 of this excerpt.	2
		(iii) Describe the music heard in the final bars of this excerpt (bar 9 to end).	2
		(iv) Tchaikovsky uses three main themes in his *Romeo and Juliet Fantasy Overture*. Describe in detail how **one** of these themes is heard for the first time in this work.	3

Gerald Barry
Piano Quartet No.1

The 20th century saw a great diversity of
styles of music composition. Composers
explored and experimented with many
different timbres and techniques. The
following musical characteristics can
be found in many 20th-century or
contemporary works of Western art music:

- Regularly changing time signatures
- Atonality
- Melodic dissonance
- Unusual rhythmic patterns
- Little or no melody or melodic structures
- Non-traditional performing techniques
- Very detailed performance instructions and tempo markings

Background to *Piano Quartet No. 1*

Gerald Barry was born in Co. Clare in 1952. He studied under composer Karlheinz
Stockhausen in Germany.

Barry's *Piano Quartet No. 1* was first performed in London in 1992. The piece features
piano, violin, viola and cello and is a chamber music work. *Piano Quartet No. 1* contains
many of the typical characteristics of 20th-century contemporary music, but also reflects
the influence of traditional Irish music on Barry's work.

Barry derived inspiration for his *Piano Quartet No.1* from a number of famous Irish
melodies, as described below.

Sí Bheag, Sí Mhór (Section A)	Believed to be Turlough O'Carolan's first song (Sheebeag and Sheemore are two small hills in Co. Leitrim)
Lord Mayo's Delight (Section H)	Collected by Edward Bunting at the 1792 Belfast Harp Festival
The Last Rose of Summer (Section C)	A poem written by Thomas Moore, set to a melody collected by Bunting at the 1792 Belfast Harp Festival
Beidh Aonach Amárach (Section F)	A popular traditional Irish folk song

Key Words

Compositional Techniques

Canon	Melody played in strict imitation between two or more parts, at a fixed distance.
Inversion	Turning a melody upside-down.
Counterpoint	Where two or more parts are playing an independent melody line.
Wedging	The intervals between notes in the original melody are stretched or widened.
Splicing	The intervals between notes in the original melody are reduced.
Augmentation	The note values of the original melody are lengthened.
Diminution	The note values in the original tune are shortened.
Telescoping	Fragments of different sections or tunes are put together to make a new section.

Performance Techniques

Open string		No fingers on the fingerboard.
Senza vibrato		Do not vibrate the string.
Harmonics		String players touch the string very lightly. This creates a very light airy sound. The diamond shape represents the harmonic.
Double stopping		Playing two notes together on a string instrument.
Détaché		Give every note a distinct separate bowing.
Note clusters		Sounding of all the notes on the piano between two indicated notes.

Flautando		Bowing very lightly over the fingerboard to create a flute-like sound.
8va over the treble stave		Play an octave higher than written.
8va under the bass stave		Play an octave lower than written.

Features of Twentieth-Century Music in *Piano Quartet No. 1*

Students are regularly asked to identify style features of the set work. If you are asked to identify features of 20th-century music in Barry's work, you should be able to list the following points and refer to the section of the work in which they are evident.

Extreme changes in dynamics. This is heard at the end of the piano solo (C4) to the start of C5: *fff* to *mp*.

Very precise tempo markings to each section. All sections are given their own specific tempo marking, for example, Section A = ♩. = 108.

Very precise performance instructions, *for example roughly, senza vibrato on violin* and viola in section B1.

Dissonance by doubling parts at a distance of a second, fourth, fifth or seventh. This can be heard in the B2 section on the strings and the piano.

Repeating themes and transforming them completely by altering texture, melodic shape, rhythm, dynamics and tempo. This is heard throughout all of the C sections.

Regularly changing time signatures in the C1 section.

Form

- There are 18 sections in the *Piano Quartet No.1*.
- Form follows an unconventional pattern.
- There is a **recurring C section**, which can be heard nine times.
- Section A is heard only once at the start of the piece.
- The piece ends with new material.

Structure

Section	1	2	3	4	5	6	7	8	9
	A	B1	C1	C2	B2	C3	D1	D2+B3	E1

Section	10	11	12	13	14	15	16	17	18
	C4	C5	E2+D3	C6	C7	F+C8	C9	G	H

Original Appearance of Themes

Section A: Bars 1–52

Section A is derived from the Irish melody *Sí Bheag, Sí Mhór* by Turlough O'Carolan, shown here:

The tune is inverted in the left hand of the piano part, starting on the note E:

There is a four-part canon at the octave, one crotchet-distance apart, played by violin, viola, cello and piano left hand.

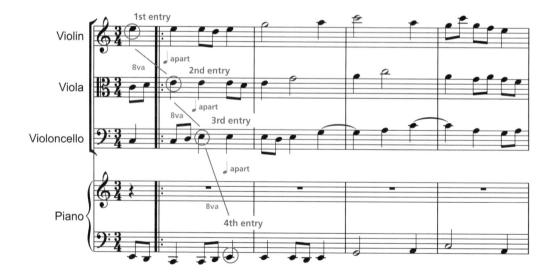

The piece then moves to a five-part canon, with the addition of piano right hand.

FEATURES

- AABB form with *f, mp, f, ff* dynamics
- Mostly in 3/4 time
- Key of C major
- Polyphonic texture

Section B: Bars 53–107

The accompaniment has a two-note drone sound, which is based on a medieval instrument called the **hurdy-gurdy**.

FEATURES

- Melody in 3/4 time
- Homophonic texture
- Key of C major with recurring C♯ notes
- Played 'roughly'

Section B is played three times:

1st appearance of Section B	Bar 53	• Melody on violin • Accompaniment on viola (hurdy-gurdy-like notes of C and G)
2nd appearance of Section B	Bar 71	• Violin and viola repeat melody and accompaniment • Cello joins playing the inversion of the viola accompaniment
3rd appearance of Section B	Bar 89	• Melody played by violin, viola and cello an octave apart • Piano plays the melody in note clusters • Violin playing two octaves higher than on the original appearance • *fff* dynamics • No C/G accompaniment

Section C: Bars 108–138

The melody in Section C is derived from the old folk tune, *The Last Rose of Summer*:

Section C of *Piano Quartet No. 1* contains two distinct melodies: one played on the violin and one on the viola.

FEATURES

- Polyphonic texture
- C melodies are heard twice
- A♭ tonal centre
- Frequent changes in time signatures

The melodies in Section C are played twice:

1st appearance of Section C melody	Bar 108	• Melody 1 on violin • Melody 2 on viola • Cello plays harmonics *pp* • Instruments play *senza vibrato*
2nd appearance of Section C melody	Bar 124	• *ff* dynamics • Violin and viola play melody 1 one octave lower (violin has rests where notes are out of range) • Melody 2 on cello • Played 'roughly, savagely' • Piano plays both melodies on both hands in bass clef

Section D: Bars 319–334

The melody in Section D is derived from the Irish tune *Beidh Aonach Amárach*:

In *Piano Quartet No. 1*, this melody is played on the viola:

FEATURES

- Rhythmically driven
- Accompaniment on cello is similar to viola accompaniment from Section B
- Starts with a 1/8 time signature
- Continuously changes time signature

Section E: Bars 357–372

The violin melody is the **retrograde** of the melody in Section D2.

There is a four-part canon at the octave with the distance of a quaver, played by the violin, viola, cello and piano left hand.

Section F: Bars 490–511

Section F of *Piano Quartet No. 1* is based on a triplet rhythm, similar to the rhythm used in a traditional Irish jig.

The melody is played on the violin, while the piano plays a **retrograde** of the melody.

Polyphonic texture:

Section G: Bars 519–527

The music in Section G is based on that in F, albeit condensed into a very brief eight-bar section.

Section H: Bars 528–571

Section H is derived from the tune *Lord Mayo's Delight*:

The melody begins with a two-part canon between the viola and the cello at the unison, one crotchet-distance apart:

The second part of the tune (the **turn** in Irish dance music) becomes a three-part canon with the entry of the piano.

At bar 558, the piano drops out and the first part of the tune is played in a three-part canon.

The last note, **D**, is played on piano, which gives an unfinished effect to the end of the work.

SAMPLE EXAM QUESTION

Describe Barry's use of Irish melodies in his *Piano Quartet No. 1.*

Barry uses the Irish melody *Lord Mayo's Delight*, in the final section of the work. The tune is heard in the form of a canon, firstly on the viola and cello, then the violin and piano join in.

This question was worth three of the 10 marks for this set work in 2011.

Try to give at least three valid pieces of information for three-mark questions. Here, the sample answer described:

- the Irish melody
- the section in which it is heard
- how it is treated musically

Analysis of *Piano Quartet No. 1*

	Bar	Texture	Points of Interest
A	1	Polyphonic	See Section A (p. 44)
B1	53	Homophonic	See Section B (p. 45)
C1	108	Polyphonic	See Section C (p. 46)
C2	140	Polyphonic	Melody 1 on viola and melody 2 on cello Original intervals of melodies are **spliced** and **wedged**
B2	170	Polyphonic	**Melody played five times in canon:** 1. (170) Three-part canon at the unison and distance of one crotchet **violin–viola–cello** *ff, searingly* 2. (188) Three-part canon **violin–cello–viola**. Piano RH doubles the string parts *ff* 3. (205) Three-part canon **cello–viola–violin**. Piano doubles the string parts *ff* 4. (222) Three-part canon **on strings and piano**. Violin and viola doubled playing in parallel fifths one octave apart, piano RH and cello doubled in parallel fifths one octave apart and piano LH plays parallel fifths *mp, lightly detached articulation, bouncing* 5. (239) Repeat of previous section, cello plays a repeated D, which gives a drone effect *ff, full-bodied sound*
C3	256	Polyphonic	**Four different versions of C, with increasing dynamics and faster tempo each time:** 1. (256) Viola and cello play melodies from C2, violin plays a tune based on melody 2 *mp* 2. (272) Piano is added, playing fragments of the melody lines, some double stopping in the string parts *mf* 3. (288) Strings play at a higher pitch, piano plays both melodies in LH at the dissonant interval of a second *f* 4. (303) Violin plays at a higher pitch, piano RH enters *ff*
D1	318	Homophonic	See Section D (p. 47) *ff roughly, detached articulation*
D2+ B3	335	Polyphonic	D is played on violin and piano RH in unison B is played on viola and cello in unison and in **dimunition** Hurdy-gurdy accompaniment on piano LH in thirds At bars 343–353, the material is repeated with different time signatures
E1	357	Polyphonic	See Section E (p. 47)

	373	Homophonic	**Hommage à Horowitz**
C4			This section is inspired by the Russian virtuoso Vladimir Horowitz
			Derived from Section C material
			Solo piano
			Both hands play in octaves
			fff, octaves played with complete abandon
C5	403	Polyphonic	Altered **melody 2** of the Section C material is played in canon **violin–viola–cello, at the octave and distance of one crotchet**
			Melody is repeated
E2+ D3	426	Polyphonic	This is the only section that has a key signature (B♭ minor) *f*
			Material from Sections E and D
			E2 is played on violin and viola in unison
			D3 is played on cello and piano RH in unison
			Music is repeated at bar 442 *ff*
			Violin plays one octave higher and piano plays one octave lower on the LH
C6	458	Polyphonic	Three-part canon on violin–viola–cello at the octave and one quaver distance apart
			p, flautando, hushed, espressivo
			Slow tempo
C7	469	Polyphonic	**This does not sound like the other C sections**
			Striding ff
			Violin and viola play in canon at the octave and at one crotchet distance
			Canon is based on an inversion of C6
			Cello plays a version of Section C melody 2
			Piano doubles the string parts
			At bar 483, the tempo becomes faster and there is some double stopping on violin and viola
			Abrupt bar of silence at 490
F+C8	490	Polyphonic	See Section F (p. 48)
			Viola and cello play the Section C melodies in **augmentation** *ff*
			The piano plays a **retrograde** of Section F material
			Brittle, nervous, exaggerated staccato
			Bar rest at 512

	512		Three-part canon based on Section C melody 2 **violin–viola–cello** at the octave at a distance of one crotchet
C9			Shortest of all C sections
			Wide range in pitch between violin and cello
			Very high-pitched violin
			Slow tempo and soft dynamics
G	519	Homophonic	See Section G (p. 48)
			Very sudden entry
			Very fast tempo
			Very loud dynamics
			Notes are taken from starts and endings of each section
H	528	Polyphonic	See Section H (p. 48)
			Molto flautando
			Some notes omitted on violin when out of range

The Canon

When answering a question on canon, it is important to provide information on which instrument plays, in what order, at what interval and what distance.

Section	Parts	Order of Entry	Interval	Distance
A	4	Violin–viola–cello–piano LH	Octave	♩
	5	Piano LH–piano RH–cello–viola–violin	Octave	♩
B2	3	Violin–viola–cello Violin–cello–viola Cello–viola–violin	Unison	♩
E1	4	Piano LH–cello–viola–violin	Octave	♪
C5	3	Violin–viola–cello	Octave	♩
C9	3	Violin–viola–cello	Two octaves	♩

H	2	Viola–cello	Unison	♩
	3	Viola–cello–piano LH Violin–viola–cello		

A question on the 2018 paper asked students to describe one feature of Gerald Barry's style as heard in his *Piano Quartet No. 1.* In order to get full marks, a feature of his style and where it can be heard in the work must be stated. A sample answer is as follows:

> *A feature of Barry's compositional style is his use of retrograde. This can be heard in the E1 section.*

The marking scheme awarded one mark for the identification of the feature, and one mark for the 'elaboration' of the feature. Elaboration can be either where the feature is heard or how it is used in the quartet.

Past Exam Questions

Year	Section	Questions	Marks
2019 Q2 (10 marks)	Section F+C8 (Bars 491–511)	(i) Describe one feature of the violin music heard in the excerpt.	2
		(ii) The texture of the music in this excerpt is polyphonic. Explain with reference to the music in the excerpt.	2
		(iii) Describe two 20th-century features as used by Gerald Barry in this excerpt.	2+2
		(iv) Identify two features of the music which immediately follow the music in this excerpt in *Piano Quartet No. 1* by Gerald Barry.	1+1
2018 Q3 (10 marks)	Section C2 (Bars 140–169)	(i) Name the instruments that play in this excerpt.	0.5+0.5

		(ii) The music performed is *mp senza vib.* Explain *mp senza vib.*	1
		(iii) An outline score of bars 1–6 of the excerpt is printed below. Insert the missing time signatures in bars 4 and 5.	0.5+0.5
		(iv) Describe the texture of the music heard in this excerpt.	2
		(v) Describe two ways in which the thematic material heard in this excerpt differs from the first time it is heard in this quartet. Refer to both sections in your answer.	1.5+1.5
		(vi) Other than texture, describe one feature of Gerald Barry's style as heard in his *Piano Quartet No.1.*	2
2017 Q1 (25 marks)	Excerpt 1: Section A (Bars 1–26)	(i) This excerpt is taken from: (multiple choice).	1
		(ii) Name the Irish tune on which the melody of this section is based.	2
		(iii) Identify the compositional technique used in this excerpt: (multiple choice).	1
		(iv) Describe how this technique is used in the excerpt.	3
		(v) Bars 1–26 are repeated in this excerpt. This repeat features a change in: (multiple choice).	1
	Excerpt 2: Section C4 (Bars 373–402)	(i) Name the section of the work that you hear in the excerpt.	2
		(ii) Describe two ways in which the music differs in this excerpt from the music in excerpt 1.	2+2
		(iii) The music of this excerpt features: (multiple choice).	2
	Excerpt 3: Section C6 (Bars 458–468)	(i) Name the three instruments heard in this excerpt.	0.5+0.5 +0.5
		(ii) In this excerpt, the performers are asked to play *flautando.* Explain.	1

		(iii) The tonality of the music in this excerpt is: (multiple choice).	1
		(iv) What effect do the changing time signatures have on the music in this excerpt?	1.5
		(v) Briefly describe any two of the following features as used in *Piano Quartet No. 1*: polymetry, augmentation, retrograde, inversion.	2+2
2013 Q3 (10 marks)	Section H (Bars 528–end)	(i) The excerpt is taken from the beginning, middle or end of the work?	1
		(ii) Name the two instruments playing at the beginning of this excerpt. Do they play *senza vibrato, espressivo or molto flautando*?	0.5+0.5 1
		(iii) Name one compositional feature used in this excerpt. Describe how this technique is used in this excerpt.	1 2
		(iv) Insert the missing time signatures at **X** and **Y** on the score.	0.5+0.5
		(v) Identify three features of Gerald Barry's musical style as heard in his *Piano Quartet No. 1*.	1+1+1

Queen
Bohemian Rhapsody

The British rock band Queen are one of the most famous and successful rock bands of all time. The original band members are Freddie Mercury (vocals), Brian May (lead guitar), John Deacon (bass guitar) and Roger Taylor (drums). They were formed in London in 1970 and have had many worldwide hits including *Killer Queen*, *Another One Bites the Dust*, *We Will Rock You* and *Radio GaGa*. However, the band are most famous for the hit *Bohemian Rhapsody*.

In October 1975, Queen released *Bohemian Rhapsody* for the first time. The single, which was accompanied by a ground-breaking promotional video, was taken from the album *A Night at the Opera*, produced by Roy Thomas Baker. The single reached the top of the UK charts in November 1975 and remained there for nine weeks.

THE BAND	
Freddie Mercury	**Composer**, vocals, piano
Brian May	Lead guitar, vocals
John Deacon	Bass guitar, vocals
Roger Taylor	Drums, vocals

How Do We Study *Bohemian Rhapsody*?

As with the other set works on your course, it is vital that you actively listen to the song. It is part of the listening paper, and you will be examined on features that you hear in the given excerpt.

It is important that you can explain all of the compositional features used in the work and can give examples of where they can be found in the song.

Revision of *Bohemian Rhapsody* should focus on the following:

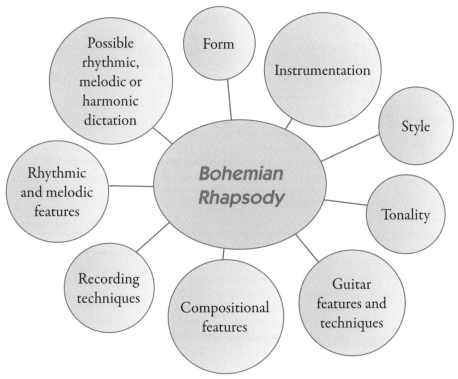

Structure and Style

The song has an unusual structure and does not have a chorus.

Section	Bar	Tonality	Instrumentation
Intro	1	B♭ major	**Lead vocals:** Freddie Mercury
Main vocal section (Verses 1 and 2)	15	B♭ major, E♭ major	**Piano:** Freddie Mercury **Electric lead guitar:** Brian May
Guitar interlude	47	E♭ major	**Electric bass guitar:** John Deacon
Operatic section	55	A major, A♭ major	**Percussion:** Roger Taylor **Operatic vocals:** Freddie Mercury,
Rock section	96	E♭ major	Brian May, Roger Taylor
Outro	123	E♭ major	

There are sudden, unexpected changes of style throughout the song. The styles can be categorised as:

- Ballad
- Operatic
- Rock

The time signature is mostly 4/4, with some brief changes throughout.

Key Words

Recording Techniques

Multi-tracking	Layering of vocal or instrumental tracks to create a choral effect from only one singer (opening bars), or an ensemble effect from only one player (rock section).
Overdubbing	Different sounds coming from different speakers or moving the sound from speaker to speaker.
Panning	Mixing two identical recordings and slowing down one of them. The sound waves are put out of sync, resulting in a 'whooshing' sound.
Flanging	An echo effect.
Reverberation	Overloading the sound to create a grittiness. This is common in rock music and can be achieved using a guitar pedal or in the recording studio.
Distortion	Process of recording vocals/instruments onto individual tracks, then mixing these into one single track.
Bouncing	The note values in the original tune are shortened.

Vocal Features

Falsetto	A male vocalist singing in an artificially high register.
A cappella	Singing unaccompanied.
Vibrato	A slight vibration in the notes that warms the tone of the vocal.

Guitar Features and Techniques

Hammer on	Playing a note with finger on the fretboard.
Glissando	Sliding from one note to another note.
Bending	Altering the pitch of the note by literally bending the string.
Vibrato	Shaking the finger on the string, causing the string to vibrate (similar to vibrato on a violin).
Power chords	Playing a chord where the third note is omitted, playing only the root note and fifth note.
Riff	A short musical figure that is repeated throughout the song (similar to an ostinato).
Lick	A short, decorated guitar passage that can be used to link two sections of a song.

Melodic Features

Repeated notes	More than one note repeated.
Chromatic movement	Pitch moves up or down in semitones.
Step movement	Pitch moves up or down by step.
Wide range	Large distance between the lowest and highest notes.

Rhythmic Features

Syncopation	Emphasis is placed on the weak beat.
Standard backbeat	Standard rock drum beat in 4/4 time.
Triplet rhythm	Three notes played in the time of two notes.

Compositional Features

Modulation	Key change within a piece.
Sequence	A musical pattern repeated at a different pitch.
Antiphony	Call-and-response technique used in opera.
Word-painting	Music is used to represent a lyric or text.

exam TIPS

Almost the entire song is in 4/4 time. There are two bars of 2/4 time in the song. A changing time signature can be described as a rhythmic feature.

Styles in *Bohemian Rhapsody*

Style	Features
Ballad	Slow tempo

Operatic	Use of operatic vocal styles such as falsetto and antiphony
	References to operatic characters such as Figaro from Mozart's *The Marriage of Figaro*
	Classical piano accompaniment
Rock	Instrumentation
	Heavy guitar and drums
	Recording and guitar techniques such as distortion and overdubbing
	Syncopated vocals and accompaniment

Word-painting

Word-painting is used throughout *Bohemian Rhapsody* so it is important to be familiar with it. Some examples are explained below.

Section	Lyrics Reference	Technique
Intro	'Little high, little low'	Panning
Intro	'Any way the wind blows'	Flange sound on cymbal
Main song, verse 2	'Sent shivers down my spine'	Bell tree effect on guitar
Operatic section	'Thunderbolt and lightning'	Rhythm punctuated on drums

Analysis of *Bohemian Rhapsody*

Introduction: Bars 1–14

Bar	Points of Interest
1	**A cappella** singing
	Four-part close harmony
	Repeated notes
	Syncopated rhythm
	Changing time signature, 4/4 to 5/4

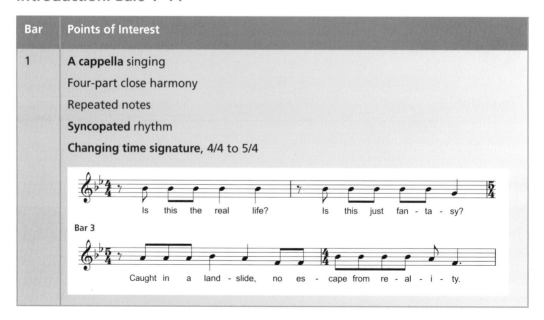

| 5 | Piano enters playing broken chords
Vocals in harmony
Piano riff (motif A) heard for the first time in bar 7
Bar 8: solo voice with countermelody in backing vocals
Bar 10: 'easy come' – chromatic vocal motif
Bar 11: panning on 'little high, little low' gives the effect of 'high' and 'low'
Bar 12: word-painting on 'wind blows' created by flanged crash cymbal (see word-painting on p. 60)
Bars 14–15: V–I cadence in B♭ major |

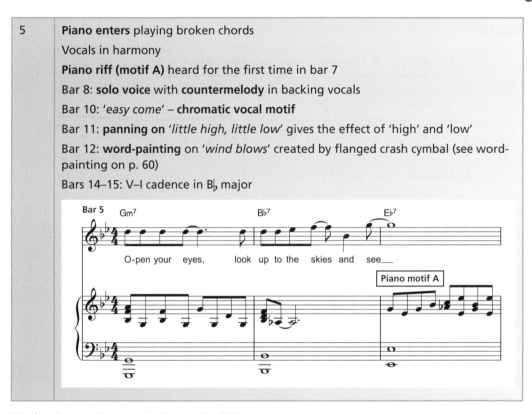

Main Song, Verse 1: Bars 15–34

Bar	Points of Interest
15	Two-bar intro on piano (piano riff/motif B)
17	Solo vocal and piano Chord progression: B♭–Gm–Cm–Cm7– F7 (I–vi–ii–ii7–V7) Bar 20: glissando on bass

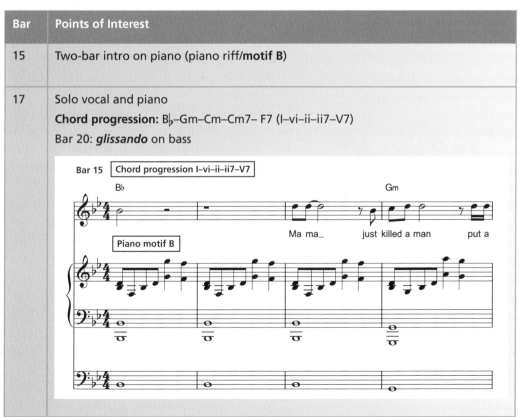

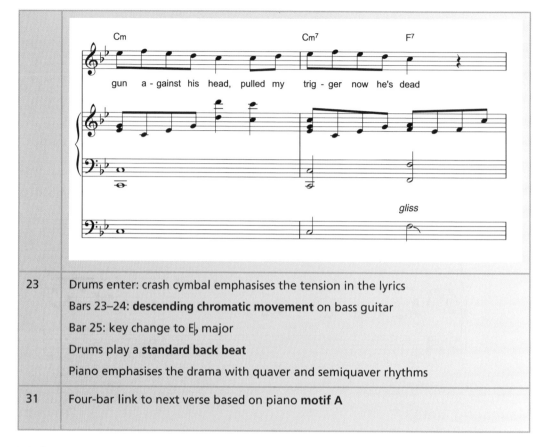

Bar	
23	Drums enter: crash cymbal emphasises the tension in the lyrics Bars 23–24: **descending chromatic movement** on bass guitar Bar 25: key change to E♭ major Drums play a **standard back beat** Piano emphasises the drama with quaver and semiquaver rhythms
31	Four-bar link to next verse based on piano **motif A**

Main song, Verse 2: Bars 35–46

Bar	Points of Interest
35	Returns to the key of B♭ major Same melody as verse 1 Drums play from the start of verse 2 **Word-painting** on *'shivers down my spine'*, created by a bell tree effect played on guitar
43	Bar 42: electric guitar enters (overdubbed). The aggressive guitar sound emphasises the mood of the lyrics **Harmonic riff:** I–V♭–vi–ii–V7 Bar 43: **backing vocals enter** Bar 46: angry mood is reflected in build-up in dynamics, emphasis on crash cymbal and semiquaver in piano and drums

Guitar Interlude: Bars 47–58

Bar	Points of Interest
47	Guitar improvises over harmonic riff from verse 2
	Piano, bass, overdubbed guitar, drums in accompaniment
	Overdubbing on guitar
	Guitar techniques: bends, vibrato, hammer on notes, glissandi, power chords
	Features of guitar solo: sequences, scalic movement, triplets, quintuplets
	Bar 53: **descending chromatic line** leads to new key and complete change in mood

Operatic Section: Bars 59–94

Bar	Points of Interest
55	Change of mood, tempo and style
	Two bars of A major staccato chords on piano introduces vocals
	Vocals based on chromatic movement (*'easy come, easy go'*) and step movement
	Solo alternates with chorus
	Drums added to *'thunderbolt and lightning'*, emphasising lyrics
	Bar 63: **antiphony** and **falsetto** on *'Galileo'*
	Panning also used
	Octaves on piano
	Bar 66: **multi-tracking** on vocals *'Magnifico'* creates a bell effect
67	Key of E♭ major
	Chromatic melody similar to opening of opera section, only a minor third lower
	Bar 67: one bar in 2/4 time
	Bar 70: multi-tracked vocals (chorus) with bass and drums
	Bar 74: piano **motif A**

75	*'Easy come, easy go'* from the intro
	Solo vocal and chorus alternate with piano, drums and bass
	Bars 76–77: dominant/tonic *'Bismillah'*, antiphonal singing and falsetto
	Rising staccato chords on *'no, no, no'*, emphasised by crash cymbal
	Bar 92: guitar returns playing **power chords**
	Triplet rhythm on percussion and piano

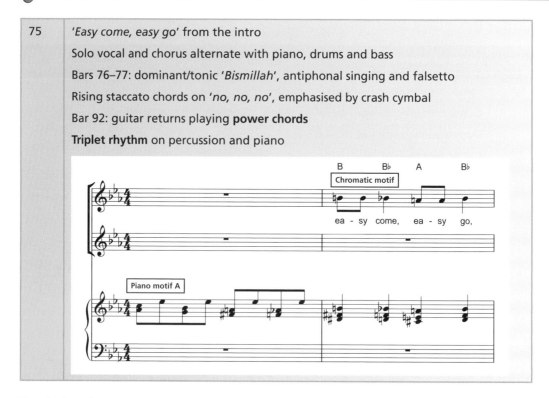

Rock Section: Bars 95–126

Bar	Points of Interest
95	Key of E♭ major
	Hard rock sound: **distortion, bends, power chords, overdubs** on guitar
	Four-bar syncopated guitar riff accompanied by bass and drums
	Bar 100: solo vocal based on triplet rhythm and repeated notes and step movement
	Bar 103: one bar of D♭ major in 2/4 time
	Bar 113: Four-bar guitar riffs from bar 96 repeated and developed
	Bar 120: tempo begins to slow and the piano returns
	Bars 122–124: overdubbed vocals

Outro: Bars 127–138

Bar	Points of Interest
127	Return to tempo of main song
	Guitar solo played over part of harmonic motif of main song (I–V♭–vi)
	Overdubbed guitar (distinctive Brian May sound)
	Melancholic mood
	Bar 128: solo voice with piano, bass and drums accompaniment
	Rubato-style singing
	Guitar drops out, followed by the bass and drums; piano left playing broken chords
	Guitar re-enters, panning on guitar
	Vocals return singing the chromatic melody 'any way the wind blows', accompanied by piano **motif A**
	Final chord of F major and a soft gong

Motifs

There are **three** motifs used throughout *Bohemian Rhapsody*. As with the other set works, you may be asked to compare or contrast the appearance of these motifs throughout the work. Motifs may also be referred to as **riffs** or **thematic material**.

Piano Motif A

- Intro: bar 7
- End of verse 1, link to verse 2: bar 32
- Operatic section: bar 74 (faster than previous appearances)
- Outro: bar 137 ('*any way the wind blows*') played on piano

Chromatic Motif

Bar 10

Eas - y   come   eas - y   go,   lit - tle   high,   lit - tle   low

- Intro: '*easy come, easy go*'.
- Operatic section: based on the chromatic motif and used throughout.
- Outro: ('*any way the wind blows*') This vocal line is a variation of the original motif.

Piano Motif B

- This motif is played throughout the main song.

SAMPLE EXAM QUESTION

Compare and contrast the music of verse 1 and verse 2 in *Bohemian Rhapsody*.

Answer

Verse 1	Verse 2
B♭ major with modulation to E♭ major	B♭ major with modulation to E♭ major
Piano and bass throughout	Piano and bass throughout
Drums enter halfway through verse	Drums heard from start of verse
No electric guitar	Electric guitar heard halfway through verse
Ends with a broken chord on piano and a return to B♭ major	Ends with a guitar solo in E♭ major

Keep your answer concise and clear. If the question asks about two different parts of a song, be sure to reference each section.

SAMPLE EXAM QUESTION

This song has been described as a 'Rock Opera'. Discuss this statement and make reference to the music.

Sample Answer

A rock opera is a piece of rock music with a dramatic story. *Bohemian Rhapsody* contains rock features, such as:

- Instrumentation (electric guitar, vocals, bass and drums)
- Standard rock backbeat In the drums heard in the main section of the song
- Recording techniques are used in the guitar solo such as distortion and reverberation.

The song also contains features that are associated with opera, such as:

- Antiphony: call-and-answer section heard between soloist and chorus (*'I'm just a poor boy nobody loves me / He's just a poor boy, from a poor family'*)
- Use of falsetto to create the effect of a soprano voice (*'Galileo'*)
- The use of Italian character names that have previously been used In Italian opera (Figaro, Bismillah, Galileo, Scaramouche)

Past Exam Questions

Year	Section	Questions	Marks
2019 Q4 (10 marks)	Operatic	**Excerpt 1**	
		(a) The opening chords of this excerpt are: (multiple choice).	1
		(b) Identify the word in the text where the drums enter for the first time in this excerpt.	1
		(c) Describe the vocal music on the word *'Magnifico'* in line 4.	2
		(d) Describe the bass line in line 7 of this excerpt.	2

		Excerpt 2	
		(e) (i) Lines 9–12 feature: (multiple choice).	1
		(ii) Explain this feature, with reference to the music heard in this excerpt.	1.5
		(f) How is the word 'no' emphasised in the music of line 13?	1.5
2018 Q2 (10 marks)	Introduction	**Excerpt 1**	
		(i) Identify two features of the vocals in lines 1–2.	1+1
		(ii) Describe one feature of the accompaniment in line 3.	2
		(iii) The music of line 5 features: (multiple choice).	1
		(iv) Identify and describe an example of word-painting, as heard in this excerpt.	1+1
		(v) Describe two differences between the music heard in this excerpt and the operatic section of *Bohemian Rhapsody*. Refer to both sections in your answer.	1.5+1.5
2017 Q2 (10 marks)	Outro	(i) Identify two features of the music heard before the main vocal line enters in this excerpt.	1+1
		(ii) Insert the five missing notes at **X** on the score.	2.5
		(iii) Describe one feature of the piano music in the last section of this excerpt (after the vocals 'nothing really matters to me' are heard).	2
		(iv) Name the percussion instrument heard at the very end of this excerpt.	0.5
		(v) Describe two differences between the music heard in this excerpt and one of the following sections of *Bohemian Rhapsody*: Opening/Main song/Operatic section.	1.5+1.5

2013 Q4 (10 marks)	Rock	(i) Identify the style of the music heard in this excerpt.	1
		(ii) Describe the music played by the guitar in the opening bars of this excerpt (before the voice enters).	2
		(iii) Identify **two** features of the vocal line in this excerpt.	1+1
		(iv) Describe an example of word-painting in this excerpt. Refer to the lyrics in your answer.	2
		(v) Freddie Mercury referred to *Bohemian Rhapsody* as a 'mock opera'. Discuss.	3
2012 Q1 (25 marks)	Introduction	**Excerpt 1**	
		(i) Identify the style of singing heard in line 1 of this excerpt.	1.5
		(ii) In which line does the piano enter? It plays: (multiple choice).	1 1
		(iii) Identify **two** features of the vocal music as heard in line 5.	1+1
		(iv) Describe the effect used to illustrate the words 'any way the wind blows' in line 6.	2
	Main song (Ballad)	**Excerpt 2**	
		(i) Describe the bass guitar part heard in bars 1–6 of this excerpt.	2
		(ii) Insert the five missing melody notes at **X** on the score.	2.5
		(iii) Describe the style of the music heard in this excerpt.	3
	Operatic	**Excerpt 3**	
		(i) From which section of the song is this except taken?	1
		(ii) The vocals in this excerpt are: (multiple choice). Explain.	1 2
		(iii) How is the word 'no' emphasised in this excerpt?	2
		(iv) Describe two ways in which the music heard in the remainder of the song contrasts with the music heard in this excerpt.	2+2

Set Works B

Wolfgang Amadeus Mozart
Piano Concerto No. 23 in A Major, K488

Wolfgang Amadeus Mozart was born in Salzburg in 1756 and became one of the most influential composers of the Classical era (1750–1800). During his lifetime, he composed over 600 works including symphonies, choral works, opera, concertos and chamber music.

Mozart's *Piano Concerto No. 23 in A Major* was composed in 1786. This work is a **solo concerto**.

A **solo concerto** is a piece of music, usually in three or four movements, for a solo instrument with an orchestral accompaniment.

Key Words

Form

Sonata form	A piece of music with the following structure: introduction, exposition, development, recapitulation, coda.
	Also known as large-scale ABA1 form.
Sonata rondo form	Combines sonata form with rondo form. It follows an ABA structure with a various episodes between themes.
Alberti bass	A repeated broken chord pattern heard in an accompaniment.
Ternary form	ABA form.

Melodic Features

Sequence	A melody that is repeated on the same instrument at a different pitch.
Scalic movement	Ascending or descending in scales.
Chromatic movement	Notes move in semitones.
Wide leaps	A wide distance between one note and the next.
Octaves	A range of eight notes between one note and the next.
Repeated notes	Two or more notes of the same pitch played one after the other.

Harmonic Features

Block chords	Notes of a chord played simultaneously.
Broken chords	Notes of a chord played individually.
Pedal note	A note that is sustained whilst harmony changes in other instruments.
Canon	Strict imitation between two or more parts at a fixed distance interval.

Other Musical Features

Ornamentation	Embellishments to the melody or rhythm.
Cadenza	A solo passage in a work that intends to show off the skill and virtuosity of the soloist.
Circle of fifths	A chord progression where each chord is an interval of a fifth apart.
Coda	Ending of a work.
Antiphonal dialogue	Call-and-answer between instruments or voices.
Modulation	Key changes.
Codetta	Small ending within a work, normally found at the end of the exposition and before the development.
Siciliana	A melancholy melody in 6/8 or 12/8 time, usually in the minor key.

Features of Classical Music in *Piano Concert No. 23*

The Classical era in Western music refers to music from 1750 to1830. Much of Mozart's music and style of writing is a pure reflection of the Classical style of composition. Its main features include:

- Simple melodic lines, normally heard in the treble clef
- Use of the Alberti bass as an accompaniment
- Modulations to related keys
- Structured phrasing

Instrumentation

Strings	Woodwind	Brass	Other
Violin I	Flute	Horn	Piano
Violin II	Clarinet in A		
Viola	Bassoon		
Cello			
Double Bass			

Ornamentation

Trill		A note that alternates rapidly and repeatedly with the note above.
Mordent		A note that is played with in a quick motion with the note above or below.
Appoggiatura		A grace note that takes half of the value of the note it precedes.

Movement 1: Allegro

Tempo	Allegro
Key	A major
Metre	4
Form	Sonata

Sonata Form

Sonata form is a very common musical structure that was especially popular in the Classical era. Think of sonata form as a large-scale version of ABA (ternary) form.

- **Section A (exposition)** usually includes the main musical themes of the work. These musical themes (the tune) are known as **subjects**. Many composers used two main subjects, the first was usually be presented in the tonic key and the second in the dominant key.
- New musical ideas may be presented in **Section B (development)**.
- In the returning **A section (recapitulation)**, the subjects are heard again, both usually in the tonic key.

In Movement 1, Mozart uses a third subject known as the **development theme**. This theme varies throughout Section B.

Themes/Subjects

Subject I: Bars 1–8

FEATURES

- Movement in thirds
- Sequence
- Repeated notes
- A major
- Step movement
- Chromatic movement
- Staccato
- Eight-bar structure
- Tied notes

Transition Theme: Bars 18–30

FEATURES

- Repeated notes
- Descending scales
- Arpeggios at end of theme
- A major
- 12 bars
- Ends with an imperfect cadence
- Sequences
- Some semiquaver movement

Subject IIa: Bars 30–38

The music of Subject II can be subdivided into Subject IIa and Subject IIb.

FEATURES

- Starts on an upbeat
- Sequences
- Eight-bar structure
- Dotted rhythm
- Repeated notes
- Descending chromatic movement

Subject IIb: Bars 46–52

FEATURES

- Six-bar structure
- Wide leaps (bar 50)
- Dotted rhythm
- Interrupted cadence (bars 51–52)
- Syncopation (bar 49)
- Starts in D minor and moves to A major

Subject III, Development Theme: Bars 143–149

FEATURES

- Pause at start of bar 143
- Syncopation
- Six-bar structure
- Tied notes across bars
- E major
- Dotted rhythm

Structure

Orchestral exposition (A)	1–66	**Subject I**
		Transition
		Subject IIa
		Subject IIb
Piano exposition (A)	67–155	**Subject I**
		Transition
		Subject IIa
		Codetta
		Subject III
Development (B)	156–197	**Subject III**
Recapitulation (A)	198–297	**Subject I**
		Transition
		Subject IIa
		Subject IIb
		Subject III
		Transition
		Subject III
		Cadenza
Coda	298–313	Subject IIb

Analysis of Movement 1

Orchestral Exposition

	Bar	Theme	Key	Accompaniment	Points of interest
Orchestral Exposition (A)	1	Subject I on violins I	A major	Repeated tonic notes on cello and double bass Violin 2 plays in parallel thirds and sixths	G♮ in bar Ends on imperfect cadence
	9	Subject I on flutes	A major	Woodwind accompany Pedal note A on horn	Ends on V–I cadence in A major
	18	Transition theme on violins and flute	A major	Repeated notes in lower strings Tonic/dominant notes on horn	*f* dynamic Fuller texture Ends on imperfect cadence in A major
	30	Subject IIa on violins, repeated with bassoon and flute	A major	Chordal accompaniment on strings	*p* dynamic Lyrical passage
	46	Subject IIb on violins	A few bars in D minor then returns to A major	Repeated notes on low strings Pedal note on horn Parallel thirds in woodwind	Antiphony between violin 1 and flute Dynamics change from *p* to *f* Ends on a perfect cadence in A major
Piano Exposition (A)	67	Subject I on piano	A major	Alberti bass in piano LH Some string accompaniment	Decorated version of Subject I Ends with perfect cadence
	82	Transition theme on violins	A major	Similar to orchestral exposition	

Piano Exposition (A)

Bar	Theme	Key	Accompaniment	Points of interest
86	Transition theme on piano	Move to E major	Chords in strings Broken chords in piano LH	Elaborate version of transition theme Use of semiquavers in melody Descending octave on piano LH Ends on chord of V in E major
98	Subject IIa on piano	E major	Block chords on piano LH	
106	Subject IIa on violin I, flute and bassoon	E major	Chords in strings	Decorated version of Subject IIa played in octaves and semiquavers on the piano
114	Subject IIb on piano	Starts in E minor and moves to E major	Alberti bass in semiquavers on piano Pedal E on horn	Some antiphonal dialogue between piano and strings in minor key Subject IIb played in decorated form Chromatic rising triplets on piano at bar 123 Ends with a trill on piano RH
137	Codetta on flute and violin I	E major	Repeated notes in low strings	Ends on V in E major
143	Subject III on violin I	E major	Countermelody on low strings and piano	Starts with two-beat rest Contrapuntal texture Piano doubles the low strings
149	Subject III as decorated piano solo	E major	Chords on strings at bar 154	Semiquaver movement on piano Imitation between piano RH and piano LH

	Bar	Theme	Key	Accompaniment	Points of interest
Development (B)	156	Variation of Subject III, imitation between woodwind and piano	Starts in E minor and modulates to a number of different keys	Long notes in bassoon and horn	Starts woodwind vs strings and piano Strings play staccato notes Lots of tied notes and dotted rhythms
	164	Inversion of Subject III on flute then piano, then violins	Number of modulations through major and minor keys	Octaves on piano LH and bassoon	Canonic writing in woodwind Florid semiquavers on piano
	170	Subject III variation in imitation between clarinet vs flute	Number of modulations	Octaves on piano LH	Semiquaver movement on piano RH
	178	Variant of subject III alternating between strings and woodwind	A minor	Pedal note E on low strings, piano LH and then horn	Rising chromatic semiquaver scales on piano
	189	Decorated chordal melody on piano	E major moving to A major	Sustained chords on strings then woodwind	Use of appoggiatura on piano RH Section links end of development to recap Ends on V chord in A major Rising chromatic scale in semiquavers on piano RH

exam TIPS

The expositions (orchestral and piano) and the recapitulation are A sections, that is, the recap recalls the main subjects from the expositions. Note that Subjects I and II are presented in A major in the recap and do not modulate to E major as they do in the piano exposition.

	Bar	Theme	Key	Accompaniment	Points of interest
Recapitulation (A)	198	Subject I on violin	A major	Pedal notes in low strings Full texture in woodwind and strings	Similar to beginning of orchestral exposition
	206	Subject I on piano	A major	Alberti bass on piano LH Woodwind accompaniment Long A note on horn	Semiquaver scales on piano
	213	Transition theme on violins and flute	A major	Repeated notes in low strings	Similar to orchestral exposition
	217	Transition theme on piano	A major	Chordal accompaniment on strings	Ends on E major chord
	228	Subject IIa on piano	A major	Block chords on piano LH	Piano solo Ends on V chord in A major
	236	Subject IIa on flute	A major	Woodwind playing in parallel thirds and sixths Block chords on strings	Decorated version of Subject IIa on piano in semiquavers and octaves
	244	Subject IIb on piano	D minor to A major to F# minor	Alberti bass on piano LH Pedal note A on horn	Antiphonal dialogue between piano and flute and violins Dialogue between violin I and piano Ends abruptly on chord V in A major

	Bar	Theme	Key	Accompaniment	Points of interest
Recapitulation (A)	261	Subject III on piano then woodwind	A major	Pedal note E on horn and low strings	Imitation between piano RH and piano LH Imitation between clarinets and bassoons Semiquaver movement on piano Trill on piano Ends with imperfect cadence in A major
	284	Transition theme on violins and flute	A major	Repeated notes Repeated A on horn	Short version of the transition theme
	290	Subject III on violin, flute and bassoon	A major	Repeated A on horn	Shortened version of Subject III Ends with a *fermata* (pause)
	297	Cadenza	Starts in E major and ends in the key of A major	Block chords on piano LH	Semiquaver movement Step movement Chromatic movement Ornamentation Virtuosic playing Triplets and sextuplets in semiquavers Ends on an extended trill on note B and V7 chord in A major
Coda	298	Subject IIb on violins	A major	Crotchet and minim movement in woodwind Parallel thirds on clarinets and bassoons	Introduced by ascending chromatic scale on violins Rising A major broken chords in low strings and horn Short canon between woodwind and violin I at bar 310 Ends on a perfect cadence in A major

Movement 2: Adagio

Tempo	Adagio
Key	F# minor
Metre	2
Time Signature	6/8
Form	ABA
Style	Siciliana

Themes

There are **four musical themes** (or subjects) in Movement 2.

Theme 1: Bars 1–12

FEATURES

- Key of F# minor
- Dotted rhythm
- Step movement
- Syncopated rhythm
- Wide leaps
- Use of rests
- Chromatic movement
- Tied notes
- Repeated notes
- G major broken chord
- Range of two octaves
- Grace notes

Theme 2: Bars 12–20

FEATURES

- Tied notes
- Step movement
- Sequences
- Simple rhythm
- F# minor
- Chromatic movement
- Syncopated rhythm
- Wide leaps
- Melody played in canon

Theme 3: Bars 20–26

FEATURES

- Repeated notes
- Chromatic movement
- Wide leaps
- F# minor
- Ornamented rhythm
- Modulation to A major
- Dotted rhythm
- Semiquavers
- Appoggiaturas

Theme 4: Bars 35–38

FEATURES

- Chromatic movement
- Step movement
- Interval of third at start
- A major
- Rising scales
- Use of rests
- Eight-bar structure
- Repeated notes
- Appoggiaturas

Structure

Section A	Theme 1 as piano solo
F# minor	Theme 2 as a canon involving violin, bassoon and flute
	Theme 3 as piano solo
Section B	Theme 4 is heard twice:
A major	• first on woodwind • second on piano

| Section A | Theme 1 extended with interrupted cadence |
| F# minor | Theme 2 heard again |

Coda	Sparse new melody on the piano
F# minor	Pizzicato strings
	Hints of theme 2
	Ends on chord of F# minor

Analysis of Movement 2

exam TIPS

To answer a question on canon correctly you must refer to:
- who is playing
- at what **pitch** they are playing
- at what **distance** they are playing

Bar	Theme	Key	Accompaniment	Points of interest
Section A				
1	Theme I as piano solo	F# minor	Block chords on piano LH	Style of a Siciliana Mood is melancholic and sombre Chord of G major in bars 9 and 10 Use of rests ic–V7–i ending
12	Theme II on violin I, clarinet, flute and bassoon	F# minor	Alberti bass in semiquavers on violin II Low strings play quavers on the first and fourth beats Pedal note (dominant) C# on violas	Canon Dynamics change from p to f Ends on perfect cadence in F# minor
20	Theme III on solo piano with orchestra joining in accompaniment	F# minor A major for repeat of theme III	Block chords on piano LH Sustained block chords on strings Pedal note E (moving to A major) at bar 28	Theme III is more decorated in melody than the other subjects Mix of legato and staccato playing on piano Ends on imperfect cadence in A major

Section A

exam TIPS

The chord progression ic–V7–i is used as a finished cadence point. The fifth of the chord of i is used as the bass note. This is called a 2nd inversion chord.

Chord i = F♯ minor (F♯, A, C♯)

Chord V7 = C♯7 (C♯, E♯, G♯, B)

exam TIPS

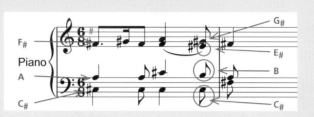

Mozart presents the Alberti bass in several different ways in Movement 2. Be familiar with who plays it and how they play it.

	Bar	Theme	Key	Accompaniment	Points of interest
Section B	*Section B*				
Section B	35	Subject IV on flute	A major	Parallel thirds on clarinet I Alberti bass in triplets on clarinet II	Tonic/dominant on horn Antiphonal dialogue between woodwind and piano
Section B	39	Subject IV piano/ flute/ clarinet		Alberti bass in triplets moves to the piano left hand	Antiphonal dialogue moves to piano and strings vs woodwind Octave leaps in flute moves music to F♯ minor Ends on imperfect cadence in F♯ minor

exam TIPS

The V–VI cadence in bars 63–64 is a notable change in the presentation of subject I from its first appearance at the start of the movement.

	Bar	Theme	Key	Accompaniment	Points of interest
		Section A			
Section A	53	Subject I on piano	F# minor	Block chords on the piano Sustained D major block chord on woodwind at bar 64	Four bars longer than the first appearance of subject I
Section A	68	Subject II on violin I and clarinet, flute vs bassoon (playing in imitation)	F# minor	Alberti bass in semiquavers on violin II Low strings play quavers on the first and fourth beats Pedal note (dominant) C# on violas	Canon Dynamics change from *p* to *f* Ends on perfect cadence in F# minor
Coda	84	New melody heard on the piano based on wide leaps	F# minor	Syncopated pizzicato broken chords on violins I and II Pizzicato broken chords on low strings	Soft dynamics Sustained block chords heard on the woodwind instruments
Coda	92	Subject II on flute, answered by a short phrase on piano	F# minor	Alberti bass played in semiquavers on violin I Low strings play quavers on first and fourth beats	Piano phrase includes octave leaps, repeated notes and a broken chord Woodwind play motif from subject II near end Ends *pp* on a repeated F# minor chord

Movement 3: Allegro assai

Tempo	Allegro assai: very fast
Key	A major
Metre	Cut common time 2/2
Form	Sonata rondo

exam TIPS

Be familiar with how to explain sonata rondo form with references to the music.

Sonata rondo form is a fusion of **two** types of form.

Traditional sonata form:	Exposition (A)	Subject I (tonic)
		Subject II (dominant key)
	Development (B)	New material derived from music from the exposition. The composer explores a variety of keys and instrumentation.
+	Recapitulation (A)	Return of subjects from exposition in tonic key

Traditional rondo form: A B A1 C A2 D A3 ...

=

Sonata rondo form in Movement 3:

Subject I is subdivided into **three** musical themes: Ia, Ib and Ic.

Subject II is subdivided into **two** musical themes: IIa and IIb.

Subjects I and II appear in exposition and recapitulation (as in sonata form).

Different versions of **Subject I** keep returning (as in rondo form).

Different thematic material in the **middle** of the work (the development section of sonata form), which is divided into two **episodes**.

Structure

Section (sonata form / rondo form)	Subject
Exposition (Subjects I and II / ABA)	**Subject Ia**
	Subject Ib
	Transition theme
	Subject Ic
	Subject IIa
	Subject IIb
	Subject Ia
Development (New thematic material / C)	**Episode 1**
	Episode 2
Recapitulation (Subjects I and II / ABA)	**Subject Ic**
	Subject IIb
	Subject Ia
	Subject Ib
	Subject IIb
Coda (Coda / Coda)	Transition theme

Subjects

Subject Ia: Bars 1–8

FEATURES

- A major
- Leap of a fifth
- Second half of phrase is the same as opening bars

- Eight-bar phrase
- Octave leap
- Use of rests
- Descending scale

- Grace note in bar 6
- Ends on perfect cadence

Subject Ib: Bars 16-20

FEATURES

- Repeated notes
- Sequences

- A major
- Starts on upbeat

Subject Ic: Bars 62–69

FEATURES

- Eight-bar structure
- Use of staccato notes

- A major
- Descending scale

- Grace note in bar 66
- Ends on an imperfect cadence

Subject IIa: Bars 106–113

FEATURES

- E minor
- Eight-bar structure
- Repeated notes
- Ends on a perfect cadence in E minor

Subject IIb: Bars 176–181

FEATURES

- E major
- Ascending and descending scale
- 12-bar phrase
- Repeated notes

Themes heard in the development section are called **episodes**. They are only heard in the development/B section and, unlike subjects, do not return in later sections.

Episode 1: Bars 230–233

FEATURES

- F# minor
- Chromatic movement
- Eight-bar melody
- Sequences
- Step movement
- Ends on an imperfect cadence

Episode 2: Bars 262–269

FEATURES

- D major
- Repeated notes
- Eight-bar phrase
- Appoggiatura in bar 273
- Mostly crotchet movement
- Ends on an imperfect cadence

Analysis of Movement 3

	Bar	Theme	Key	Accompaniment	Points of interest
Exposition		*Subject I and II (A)*			
	1	Subject Ia on piano	A major	Alberti bass on piano LH	A major scale in bar 8
	9	Subject Ia on violin I	A major	Woodwind play chordal accompaniment Alberti bass in violin II Repeated notes (pedal A) in low strings	*Tutti* (everyone plays) section
	16	Subject Ib on violin I, answered by contrapuntal melody on woodwind	A major	Strings harmonising with similar rhythmic patter as violin I	Change of texture from homophonic to polyphonic Bassoon countermelody at bar 28 Syncopated rhythm on violins at bar 35
	40	Transition theme on violin I	A major	Repeated notes on violin II and viola	Parallel thirds on bassoons and clarinets at bars 46–49 Triplet semiquavers on violins at bars 52
	62	Subject Ic on solo piano	A major	Block chords and parallel thirds on piano LH	Grace notes at bar 66
	70	Subject Ic on clarinet I	A major	Parallel thirds on clarinet II Pedal A on horn	Scales and turns on the piano from bar 74 Music moves to the key of E major (dominant) Chromatic scales on piano Block chords on strings from bar 77 Ends with a trill on piano
		Subjects I and II (B)			
	106	Subject IIa on flute	E minor	Semibreves on low strings Alberti bass in violin II Pedal note in viola	Flute and bassoon play in parallel thirds

Exposition	114	Subject IIa on piano	E minor	Alberti bass on piano LH Sustained chords on strings	Decorated version of Subject IIb Ascending chromatic movement at bar 125
	129	Codetta	E major	Broken chords on piano LH Descending scale on strings Descending scale in octaves on piano LH at bar 163	Music moves towards E major Lots of fast scale passages on piano Ends with a trill
	176	Subject IIb on piano	E major	Pizzicato notes on strings Alberti bass on piano LH Pedal note B on horn	No low strings
	182	Subject IIb on flute, clarinet and bassoon	E major	Pedal note B on horn Alberti bass on piano LH	Countermelody heard on piano Several V–I cadences in E major Ends in A major
Development (Rondo C)	*Subjects I and II (A)*				
	202	Subject Ia on piano	A major	Alberti bass on piano LH	A major scale in bar 8
	210	Subject Ia on violin I	A major with minor key modulations	*Tutti* Similar accompaniment to music at bar 9 Repeated crotchet notes in low strings	Music moves through several different keys Strong ending on imperfect cadence in F♯ minor
	230	Episode 1 on piano	F♯ minor	Sustained chords on strings Contrapuntal section on woodwind at bar 238	Section opens on strong F♯ minor chord Pedal note C♯ on horn
	246	Episode 1 on piano	Starts on F♯ minor, several modulations	Contrapuntal section on woodwind moves the music towards D major	Pedal note A on horn (dominant of D major)

262	Episode 2 on clarinets I and II	D major	Alberti bass on piano LH	Flute plays second half of episode
270	Episode 2 on piano	D major	Alberti bass moves from piano LH to RH Parallel thirds on clarinet and bassoon	Dialogue between woodwind and piano Rising sequences on piano Ends on imperfect cadence in A major

Subjects I and II (A)

312	Subject Ic on piano	A major	Block chords and parallel thirds on piano LH	Use of turns and grace notes in melody
320	Subject Ic on flute and bassoon	A minor	Pedal note A on horn Piano plays parallel thirds	Dialogue between piano, strings and woodwind

Subjects I and II (B)

330	Subject IIa on flute	A major	Long notes on low strings Pedal note E on horn	Ends on a perfect cadence in A major
338	Subject IIa on piano	A minor	Sustained chords on strings Alberti bass on piano LH Long tied notes in low strings	Dialogue between piano and woodwind Several modulations Ends on perfect cadence in A major
364	Codetta from exposition	A major	Repeat of bars 129–175	
412	Subject IIb on piano; clarinet and bassoon take over melody at bar 418	A major	Octave leaps on piano LH Pedal note A on horn Pizzicato crotchets on strings	Similar to Subject IIb at bars 176–187 Rising and falling scales on piano

Recapitulation

Recapitulation	Subjects I and II (A)				
	441	Subject Ia on piano; violins take over melody at bar 449	A major	Same as music from the start of the movement	Rising chromatic scale on piano at bar 448 End on perfect cadence in A major
	456	Subject Ib on violin	A major	Contrapuntal melody on woodwind Strings play a similar rhythm	Piano plays a decorated version of Subject Ib at bar 464
	Subjects I and II (B)				
	481	Subject IIb	D major	Pedal note A on horn Alberti bass on piano left hand Pizzicato strings	Woodwind play melody at bar 489 Piano plays countermelody against woodwind

exam TIPS

When studying the differences between the exposition and the recapitulation, think about the key centres and instrumentation. For example:

Exposition:

- A major with modulations to E minor and E major
- Opens with Subject Ia on piano

Recapitulation:

- Mostly in A major, with modulations to A minor and D major
- Opens with Subject Ic on piano

	Bar	Theme	Key	Accompaniment	Points of interest
Coda	496	Transition theme on violin I and flutes	A major	Repeated quaver notes on violin II and viola	Horn plays in imitation against the violins and flutes Tied notes and syncopation heard in melody Ends on a repeated A major chord

Common Keys Used in *Piano Concerto No. 23*

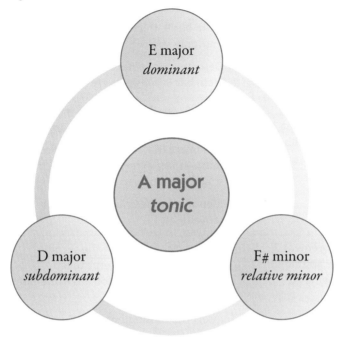

E major
dominant

A major
tonic

D major
subdominant

F# minor
relative minor

Past Exam Questions

exam Q

Year	Excerpt	Questions	Marks
2016 Q1 (25 marks)	Excerpt 1: Movement 3, Exposition, Subject Ia	*Full excerpt* (i) From which section of the movement is this excerpt taken? The tempo is: (multiple choice).	3 1
		Bars 1–8 (ii) Identify one feature of the melody in this excerpt.	1
		(iii) Describe one feature of the accompaniment in this excerpt.	2
		(iv) The excerpt ends with: (multiple choice).	1
		Bars 9–16 (v) Describe one way in which the music of bars 9–16 differs from the music of bars 1–8.	2
		(vi) Name the cadence heard at the end of the excerpt.	1

	Excerpt 2: Movement 3, Subject Ic	(i) Insert the missing notes on the score.	2
		(ii) From bar 9, the melody is repeated by: (multiple choice).	1
		(iii) Describe one feature of the piano music from bar 9 in this excerpt.	2
	Excerpt 3: Movement 3, Subject IIb	(i) Identify one feature of the music played by the strings in bars 1–8 of this excerpt.	2
		(ii) The music that immediately follows the music in this excerpt is the main theme/1st subject. It is played by: (multiple choice).	2
		(iii) Identify and describe the form of this movement.	1+4
2015 Q3 (10 marks)	Movement 2, Recapitulation, Theme A	(i) From which section of the second movement is this excerpt taken? The tempo marking for this movement is: (multiple choice).	1 0.5
		(ii) Insert the missing notes at **X** on the score.	2.5
		(iii) Identify the cadence at **Y** on the score. Do not use chord symbols or Roman numerals.	2
		(iv) Describe one feature of the accompaniment in bars 1–5 of this excerpt.	2
		(v) Describe one feature of the music heard in the Coda section of this movement.	2
2014 Q1 (25 marks)	Excerpt 1: Movement 1, Piano exposition	(i) From which section of the movement is this excerpt taken?	2
		(ii) The opening bars of this excerpt feature an Alberti bass. Explain, with reference to the music heard in this excerpt.	3+1
		(iii) This excerpt begins with piano only. In which bar are more instruments added? These instruments are: (multiple choice).	1
		(iv) Identify the cadence at the end of the excerpt.	1
	Excerpt 2: Movement 1	(i) The tonality of this excerpt is: (multiple choice).	1
		(ii) Insert the eight missing melody notes at **X** on the score.	4
		(iii) Identify **two** instruments which play the melody from bar 9.	1+1
		(iv) Describe one feature of the piano music from bar 9 to the end of the excerpt.	2

Excerpt 3: Movement 1	(i)	From which section of the movement is this excerpt taken?	1
	(ii)	Which **two** of the following can be heard in this excerpt? (multiple choice)	1+1
	(iii)	Describe one way in which the music played by the soloist contrasts with the music played by the orchestra in this excerpt.	2
	(iv)	Identify and describe the form of this movement.	2

Hector Berlioz
Symphonie Fantastique Op. 14

Background to *Symphonie Fantastique*

French Romantic composer Hector Berlioz composed the *Symphonie Fantastique* in 1830. This large-scale work in five movements tells the story of an artist who poisons himself with opium because of unrequited love.

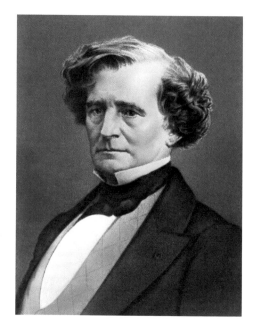

This style of writing in this work is known as **programme music**. Programme music is instrumental music that captures an emotion, image or story, and was very popular in the mid-19th century.

This work is a 'fantasy' in which Berlioz brings the listener on an emotional journey from the first time the artist sees the object of his affection, through feelings of intense love to the darkness of his belief that his love is unreciprocated, culminating in the artist poisoning himself with opium and dreaming that he has killed his beloved.

Berlioz uses a recurring theme throughout the work to represent his beloved. This recurring theme is called the **idée fixe** (fixed idea). It appears in all five movements of the work.

Students are required to study the music of Movement 2 and Movement 4 for the Leaving Certificate exam.

Key Words

Symphony	A work for orchestra usually in three or four movements.
Movement	Part of a large work, e.g. a symphony or concerto.
Sonata form	A piece of music that follows a structure of: introduction, exposition, development, recapitulation, coda. Also known as large-scale ABA1 form.
Idée fixe	A melodic idea that Berlioz uses throughout *Symphonie Fantastique* to represent his beloved.
Sextuplet	Playing six notes in the same time as four. ♪♪♪♪♪♪ in the same time as ♪♪♪♪ └── 6 ──┘

Programme music	A genre of music where the music tells a story or reflects a person, place or event; descriptive without words.
Transposing instrument	An instrument that produces a different sound from the music that the player reads, e.g. a clarinet in B♭ will read the note C but play a B♭.
Rubato	Not in strict tempo.
Sequence	A musical idea that, when repeated, changes pitch.
Tremolo strings	Rapid bowing on a given note.
Inversion	A compositional feature whereby the original musical idea is played upside-down, i.e. C–D–E would become C–B♭–A♭.
Waltz	A dance in 3/4 time.
Dolce e tenero	Sweetly and tenderly.
Allegro non troppo	Lively, but not too much.
Valse	Waltz.
Allegretto non troppo	Fairly lively but not too much.
Rallentando (rall.)	Slow down.
A tempo	Back to original tempo.
Soli	Solo.
Triplet	Three notes played in the time of two notes of the same value.
Divisi	Divide a single section of the orchestra into two or more subsections. For example, the cello section plays different musical lines.
Animez	Animated.
Ophicleide	Tuba.
Poco cresc. molto	Getting much faster.
1° tempo con fuoco	The first tempo with force.

Features of Romantic Music in *Symphonie Fantastique*

This work is an excellent example of Romantic music – Western art music that covers the period in music from approximately 1800 to 1900.

Features of Romantic music found in *Symphony Fantastique* include:

Rich orchestration and timbre	Use of a large brass section in Movement 4
	Four-part harmony in double basses in Movement 4
	Use of harp throughout Movement 2
	Antiphony between the different families of instruments throughout both movements
Rich harmonies and regular key changes	The music makes a number of tonal changes at the beginning of Movement 2 before settling in the key of A major
Abrupt key changes	In Movement 2, the music moves abruptly from A major to the unrelated key of F major

Movement 2: Un Bal

The artist is placed in the most diverse of life's situations, amongst a festive crowd, in the peaceful contemplation of the beauties of nature; but everywhere, in the town, in the fields, the cherished image comes to him and troubles his soul.

FROM HECTOR BERLIOZ'S PROGRAMME NOTES

Instrumentation of Movement 2

Strings	Woodwind	Brass
Violin I	Flute ×2	Horn (in E)
Violin II	Oboe	Horn (in C)
Viola	Clarinet (in A) ×2	
Cello		
Double bass		
Harp ×2		

Tempo	*Valse; allegro non troppo* = Waltz; lively but not too much (dotted crotchet = 60)
Key	A major
Metre	3
Time Signature	3/8 (three quaver beats to a bar)
Form	Sonata

Outline of Form/Structure of Movement 2

Movement 2 follows a sonata form structure. The introduction contains a number of important features students may be asked about in the exam.

Introduction	Exposition Section A Bars 37–119	Development Section B Bars 120–174	Recapitulation Section A Bars 175–256	Coda Bars 257–end
Bars 1–36				
Tremolo strings set up A minor tonality, which moves through several key centres until music reaches A major	Subject I Subject II Subject III Subject I	Idée fixe Idée fixe with fragments of Subject I	Subject I Subject II Subject III Subject I	New two-bar melody Fragments of all three subjects Idée fixe Reference to Subject I

Subjects

Subject I: Bars 38–54

FEATURES

- A major
- Semiquaver movement
- *Rall.* in bar 49 with a return to original tempo at bar 50

- Step movement
- Chromatic movement
- Slide from one note to another in bars 43 and 51

- Starts on upbeat
- *sf*: a sudden loudness on first beat of bar 51
- Ends on perfect cadence in A major

Subject II: Bars 56–66

FEATURES

- A major
- Repeated notes
- Semiquaver triplets
- Some chromatic movement
- Mostly semiquaver and quaver movement
- Sequences
- Ends on perfect cadence in A major
- Tied notes
- Dotted rhythm in bar 64

Subject III: Bars 68–77

FEATURES

- *sf* to *p* in bars 68–69
- Repeated notes
- Descending sequence
- Mostly semiquaver movement
- Chromatic movement
- Accent on the first beat of bars 68–72

Idée fixe: Bars 120–135

FEATURES

- F major
- Starts on upbeat
- Mostly quaver movement
- Syncopated rhythm
- Tied notes
- Sequences

Analysis of Movement 2: Un Bal

	Bar	Key	Subject/Link	Accompaniment	Points of Interest
Introduction	1	A minor		Tremolo chord on the violins and viola	Played *pp*
	3	Various keys	Cellos play tremolo rising chords Double basses play in quavers	Tremolos in violins and violas	Melody answered by rising arpeggio semiquavers in triplets on harp Dynamics move from *pp* to *ff*
	32	A major	Descending scale on harp and joined by woodwind	Strings play block chords *ff* on the first beat of each bar	Parallel thirds on flutes and clarinets in A Ends on a V–I cadence in A major
	36	A major	Two-bar link on strings	Cellos and double bass play on the beat Violins II and violas play on the second and third beat of the bar	Sets up waltz rhythm and establishes key centre of A major

exam TIPS

The waltz rhythm is represented by low strings on the first beat and violins II and violas on the second and third beats.

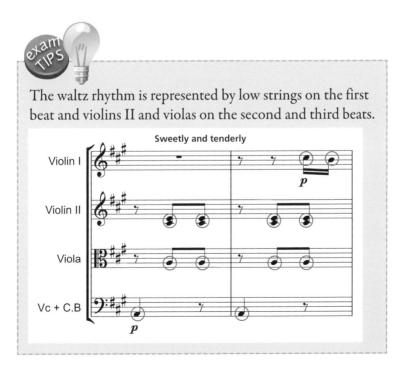

	Bar	Key	Subject/Link	Accompaniment	Points of Interest
Exposition (Section A)	37	A major	Subject I on violins I	As for bar 36 Strings play the waltz rhythm	Played *dolce e tenero* (sweet and tender) Soft dynamics Slows down at bars 49 and 50 Returns to original tempo at bar 51 Ends on perfect cadence in A major at bar 53
	54	A major	Two-bar link on harp and low strings	Repeated semiquavers on violins II and viola	Harp plays semiquaver rising arpeggios Low strings play quaver rising arpeggios
	56	A major	Subject II on violins I	Broken semiquaver chords on harp Quaver movement in lower strings	Lower strings play pizzicato Woodwind and horn block chord at bar 62 Ends on perfect cadence in A major
	66	A major	Two-bar link on woodwind	Repeated E on horn at bar 67 Parallel thirds on clarinet	Dynamic change from *p* to *f*
	68	A major	Subject III on violins I	Strings play harmony in rhythm of the melody	*sf* on first beat of bar 68
	78	A minor	Subject III extended in canon between violins I and cellos	Antiphonal dialogue between woodwind and horns Pizzicato quavers on violins II and violas	Trill on violin I and cello at bar 85 Contrary motion between violin I and cellos at bar 86 Ends on block chord of E major
	94	A major	Subject I on violins I	Waltz rhythm divided between: • First beat other strings • Second beat harp • Third beat woodwind and horns	Fuller texture than first appearance of Subject I Does not slow down Tremolos return in strings at the end of section Descending chromatic movement in the cello Dynamics move to *pppp* (*presque rien*, which means almost nothing)

If asked to describe the canon, you might need to give three pieces of information for full marks. For example:

(1) Violins I and cellos play in canon. (2) The cellos enter two beats after the violins. (3) They play an octave lower than the violins.

	Bar	Key	Subject/Link	Accompaniment	Points of Interest
Development (Section B)	120	F major	Idée fixe on flute and oboe	Tremolos on violins and violas	Dynamic marking p on melody
				Broken chords on cellos and double basses	Presence of waltz rhythm has disappeared.
	128	C major then F major	Idée fixe continued on flute and clarinet	Waltz rhythm returns on double basses, cellos and violas	Texture changes to polyphonic as fragments of Subject I heard on violins I, II and viola against the idée fixe
				Pedal note E on horns at bar 163, suggesting a move back to A major	Antiphonal dialogue between strings and woodwind at bar 163
					Ends on E major block chord at bar 174

exam TIPS

Be aware of the changes in musical features when moving from one section of the work to the next section. Students are regularly tested on their knowledge on what happens in the music after the given excerpt.

Bar	Key	Subject/Link	Accompaniment	Points of Interest
175	A major	Subject I on violins II, violas and cellos	Pizzicato repeated A notes on cellos and double basses on woodwind ♫♩	Demisemiquaver countermelody on violins I No waltz rhythm Harp enters at bar 183 No *rall.* in this appearance of subject I
191	A major	Two-bar link of rising arpeggios on harp and lower strings	Repeated semiquaver chords on woodwind	Lower strings play pizzicato quavers Harp plays semiquaver broken chords
193	A major	Subject II on violins and violas	Semiquaver broken chords on harp Repeated semiquaver chords on woodwind Quaver rising arpeggios on lower strings	Ends on perfect cadence in A major
203	A major	Two-bar link on flutes and clarinets	Parallel thirds on clarinets	Cello plays a descending semiquaver scale in contrary motion with woodwind
205	A major	Subject III on woodwind	Ascending semiquaver broken chord triplets on harp Quaver broken chords dispersed throughout the string section	Strings play pizzicato broken chords Flutes play parallel thirds Clarinets play parallel octaves
215	E minor	Subject III extended in canon of violin I against flutes, clarinets and cellos	Antiphonal dialogue between violin II and violas	Violin II and violas playing in canon Bar rest at 232
233	A major	Subject I on woodwind	Waltz rhythm in strings Violin I playing repeated notes Horns play syncopated rhythm	Harp joins in on Subject I at bar 240 *Rall.* at bar 243 Ending of Subject I repeated with *rall.*

Recapitulation (Section A)

	Bar	Key	Subject/Link	Accompaniment	Points of Interest
Coda	257	A major	New two-bar melody in woodwind (see above) which is repeated in sequences	Short descending melody in violins Tremolo on strings	Texture is polyphonic Tempo gets faster Dynamics get louder
	288	A major	Parts of main themes heard in woodwind and violin I	Waltz rhythm returns in harp, horn, clarinet and strings	Dynamics *ff*
	302	D major then A major at 309	Idée fixe on solo clarinet	Pedal note A on horn A major chord on harps at 309	Clarinet plays harmony towards end Slows down All instruments return at 320 playing *ff*
	338	A major	Subject I runs through the strings from cello to viola, to violins	Repeated notes in semiquavers on woodwind Descending scale played in tremolos on double bass	Music gets louder Ends on V–I cadence

Movement 4: March au Supplice

Convinced that his love is spurned, the artist poisons himself with opium. The dose of narcotic, while too weak to cause death, plunges him into a heavy sleep accompanied by the strangest of visions. He dreams that he has killed his beloved, that he is condemned, led to the scaffold and witnessing his own execution. The procession advances to the sound of a march that is sometimes somber and wild, and sometimes brilliant and solemn, in which a dull sound of heavy footsteps follows without transition the loudest outbursts. At the end of the march the first four bars of the Idée fixe reappear like a final thought of love interrupted by the fatal blow.

From Hector Berlioz's Programme Notes

Tempo	Allegretto non troppo
Key	G minor
Metre	2
Time signature	2/2
Form	Introduction Section A Section B Section C Coda

Instrumentation of Movement 4

Strings	Woodwind	Brass	Percussion
Violin I	Flute ×2	Horn (in B♭) basso	Timpani ×4
Violin II	Oboes ×2	Horn (in E♭)	Cymbals
Viola	Clarinets in C ×2	Trumpets (in B♭) ×2	Bass drum
Cello	Bassoons ×4	Cornets (in B♭) ×2	Snare drum
Double bass		Alto trombone	Tamburo
		Tenor trombones ×2	
		Ophicleides (tubas) ×2	

Themes

Death/Descending Theme: Bars 17–24

FEATURES

- Key of G minor
- Ascending octave leap
- Descending melodic minor scale
- Two-octave range
- Use of crotchet rests
- Ends on imperfect cadence

March Theme: Bars 62–69

FEATURES

- Key of B♭ major
- Syncopated rhythm
- Dotted rhythm
- Step movement
- Repeated notes
- Tied notes
- Descending scale
- Accented notes
- Ends on a perfect cadence

The sextuplet rhythmic motif is played on the timpanis in the opening bars of Movement 4. It can be heard on different instruments throughout the movement.

Outline of Form/Structure

Introduction	Section A	Section B	Section C	Coda
1–16	17–77	78–104	105–134	135–end
Sextuplet rhythm used in timpanis	Descending/Death theme played five times in various ways	Transition section: fragments of the March theme and sextuplets from the introduction, and the descending theme	Transition section repeated	Descending theme played by strings in inversion
Syncopated rhythm on horns	March theme played by brass and woodwind	March theme played by brass and woodwind	Descending theme played by trombones and ophicleide, then by full orchestra	Idée fixe on clarinet

This section of the work has come up in the exam papers several times. Here are some important questions to think about when studying this section:

- What instrument(s) plays the melody?
- What is happening in accompaniment?
- What key is it played in?
- Is there a countermelody?

	Bar	Key	Subject/link/motif	Accompaniment	Points of interest
Introduction	2	G minor	Syncopated melody heard on the horns ♩ 𝅗𝅥 ♩ 𝅗𝅥	Sextuplet rhythm on timpani Pizzicato notes on low strings	Dynamics start *p* Gradual build in dynamics to *ff* Ends on a dramatic chord of V7
Section A: Death/Descending theme	17	G minor	Cellos and double basses	Strings and bassoon play block chords in bars 23 and 24	First appearance of theme Opening bars are monophonic in texture Dynamics from *ff* to *p* Ends on an imperfect cadence
	25	G minor	Violas, cellos, double basses play descending theme with solo bassoon playing a countermelody	Violins I and II play chords bars 30 and 31 Sextuplet rhythm on timpanis returns at bar 32 Syncopated rhythm on horns at bar 32	Second rendition of theme Texture is contrapuntal/polyphonic *ff* dynamics at bar 40 with a syncopated melody on brass Ends on an imperfect cadence
	33	E♭ major	Violins I and II play descending theme in octaves Countermelody on violas, cellos and double basses	Sextuplet rhythm on timpanis Full orchestra in bar 40	Third rendition of theme Texture is contrapuntal/polyphonic Dynamics from *ff* to *p* Ends on an imperfect cadence in E♭ major

	Bar	Key	Subject/link/motif	Accompaniment	Points of interest
Section A: Death/Descending theme	41	E♭ major	Violins I and II play descending theme in octaves Countermelody on violas, cellos and double basses	Repeat of previous descending theme	Fourth rendition of theme Texture is contrapuntal/polyphonic Key change to G minor at bar 48 Varying dynamics
Section A: Death/Descending theme	49	G minor	Descending theme on cellos and double basses Inversion of the theme on the violas and violins Countermelody on bassoon	At bar 60, the ophicleides play B♭ quaver octaves and timpanis mark out B♭ chord	Fifth rendition of theme Strings play pizzicato Texture is contrapuntal/polyphonic Dynamics vary from *mf* to *pp*
Section A: March theme	62	B♭ major	Brass and woodwind	Steady crotchet beats on the timpanis Octave leaps on the ophicleides	At bars 69 and 77, strings mark the cadence points Some percussion Sextuplet rhythm on timpanis
Section B	78	G minor	Antiphonal dialogue between brass and woodwind	Sextuplet rhythm on the strings	Brass and woodwind dialogue is derived from the March theme
Section B	82	G minor	Descending theme played in fragments and played throughout sections of the orchestra	Some percussion Sextuplet rhythm on timpanis	Strings alternate from arco to pizzicato

	Bar	Key	Subject/link/ motif	Accompaniment	Points of interest
Section B	89	B♭ major	March theme played on brass and woodwind	Brass and woodwind instruments play in parallel thirds Dialogue between violins I and II Viola and cellos play broken chord quaver triplets Octave B♭ on ophicleide	Full orchestral texture
Section C	105	G minor	Antiphonal dialogue between brass and woodwind	Sextuplet rhythm on the strings	Brass and woodwind dialogue derived from the March theme At bar 113, descending chromatic crotchets on woodwind and strings
	114	G minor	Descending theme on brass	Ascending scales on strings with grace notes added Sextuplet melody in woodwind	Very dramatic dynamics *ff* and crescendo At bar 122, chromatic scale on woodwind in sextuplets
	115	G minor	Descending theme on brass, woodwind and lower strings	*ff* tremolos on timpanis, violins and violas Cymbals and bass drum play on the off beats	Dynamics vary from *ff* to *pp* At bar 30, all instruments play a C♯ note *ff*
	131	D♭ major	Descending theme in inversion on brass, woodwind and lower strings	*ff* tremolos on timpanis, violins and violas Cymbals and bass drum play on the off beats	Very full texture Dynamics *ff*
Coda	135	Various keys	Variation on descending theme on strings	At bar 139, a syncopated dissonant chord heard in brass and woodwind	*ff* dynamics

	Bar	Key	Subject/link/motif	Accompaniment	Points of interest
Coda	140	G minor	Dotted rhythm melody on strings	Dotted rhythm repeated note G on woodwind	At bars 143–144, a perfect cadence in G minor played on brass and woodwind
	152	G minor	Descending scale on strings followed by antiphonal dialogue between woodwind and brass, and strings	Parallel thirds and sixths in many instruments	Varying dynamics D major *ff* tremolo chord at bar 160 followed by a dramatic descending quaver triplet scale on most instruments at bar 161
	164	G major	Idée fixe on clarinet in C	Clarinet solo	Shortened version of idée fixe At bar 169, three-note pizzicato strings represent the guillotine dropping
	170	G major	No theme	Percussion play tremolo like a drumroll	Dramatic G major chords to end

exam focus

SAMPLE EXAM QUESTION

Describe how Berlioz uses the idée fixe theme throughout the movements you have studied in *Symphonie Fantastique*.

Sample answer:

The idée fixe first appears in the development of Movement 2, on the flute and oboe and then flute and clarinet. It is first heard in F major and a homophonic texture, before being heard in C major and a polyphonic texture.

The idée fixe is heard again at the end of Movement 2, in the coda. It is heard on clarinet, in A major and has a homophonic texture.

Finally, the idée fixe is heard in the coda of Movement 4. Again, it appears on clarinet, but this time in G major and with a monophonic texture.

Past Exam Questions

Year	Movement and Section	Questions	Marks
2016 Q2 (10 marks)	Movement 2: Un Bal Idée fixe (Development)	(i) Name **one** instrument which plays the theme in this excerpt.	1
		(ii) In this excerpt, the theme is first heard in the key of: (multiple choice). It is repeated in the key of: (multiple choice).	0.5 0.5
		(iii) Describe **one** feature of the accompaniment in this section.	2
		(iv) The texture of the music in this excerpt is polyphonic. Give **one** reason to support this statement.	2
		(v) What name did Berlioz give the theme in this excerpt? How does he use this theme in the movement you have studied in *Symphonie Fantastique*?	1 3

The idée fixe makes three appearances in these movements: two in Movement 2 and one in Movement 4. You may be asked how these appearances differ from each other. Consider key, instrumentation and texture in your answer.

2015 Q2 (10 marks)	Movement 4: March au Supplice Coda	(i) Identify and describe the texture of the music in bars 1–4, as heard in this excerpt: (multiple choice).	1+2
		(ii) Which two features can be heard after bar 4: (multiple choice).	2

		(iii) Name the instrument which plays the idée fixe theme in this excerpt.	1
		(iv) What is the tonality of the final chord heard in this excerpt?	2
		(v) Describe how Berlioz brings this movement to a close.	2
2014 Q3 (10 marks)	Movement 2: Un Bal Exposition	(i) In bars 1–16: Identify the instrument playing the melody. Describe the accompaniment.	3
		(ii) From bar 17 to the end of the excerpt, the music features: (multiple choice).	2
		(iii) Describe one way in which the music heard from bar 17 to the end of the excerpt differs from the music heard in bars 1–16.	2
		(iv) The final chord in this excerpt is the: (multiple choice).	1
		(v) Describe the music which immediately follows the excerpt in the movement.	2

exam TIPS

Violins I play the melody of the waltz theme in its first appearance of Un Bal. Make sure to state 'violins I' (or 'first violins') and not just 'violins' in general for full marks.

2010 Q2 (10 marks)	Movement 4: March au Supplice Exposition: Descending theme	(i) From which movement of the work is this excerpt taken?	1

		(ii) In bars 1–8: Name one instrument which plays the theme.	1
		State the range of this theme.	1
		Identify the texture of the music in these bars.	1
		(iii) Name one instrument which plays a countermelody in bars 9–16.	1
		The rhythm of this countermelody is: (multiple choice).	1
		(iv) Identify two ways in which the music of bars 17–32 differs from the music of bars 1–16.	2
		(v) Describe the music which immediately follows this excerpt.	2

exam
TIPS

Students are regularly asked to identify and describe the texture of an excerpt. Refer to the music in the excerpt for full marks.

Raymond Deane
Seachanges (with Danse Macabre)

Raymond Deane was born in Galway in
1953, brought up on Achill Island,
Co. Mayo, and graduated from UCD in
1974. He is an award-winning pianist and
a founding member of the Association of
Young Irish Composers. He studied with
composers Gerald Bennett, Karlheinz
Stockhausen and Isang Yun, and has been
a member of Aosdána – Ireland's state-
sponsored academy of creative artists –
since 1986.

In 2005, he was awarded a doctorate in
Composition by NUI Maynooth. He is
based in Dublin and Fürth.

Revising the Basics

It is very important that you are able to **discuss** *Seachanges* with regard to the following:

- The **main themes** and how they develop throughout the work
- The **form** and **tonal centres**
- **Instrumentation** – be familiar with the sound of all instruments that can be heard
- **Compositional techniques** – the definitions, where they can be heard in the work, and which instruments are involved
- **Instrumental techniques** – the definitions, where they can be heard, and which instruments they apply to
- **Unusual time signatures**
- **Mexican influences**
- **Twentieth-century musical features** and where they can be found
- The **role of percussion** throughout
- The **role of the piano** in the different sections
- The reason why the piece is named *Seachanges*
- How Deane creates a **sense of surprise** in the work
- How Deane portrays the **spirit of the Danse Macabre**

Inspiration for *Seachanges*

Deane drew inspiration for *Seachanges* from:

- **The coastline:** Deane wanted to explore the contrasting nature of the Atlantic coastline at Ardtrasna in Co. Sligo with the Pacific coastline at Huatulco in Mexico.
- **Mexican iconography:** *Seachanges* was also in part a reaction to the grotesque and gaudy portrayal of death in Mexican iconography. You can look at pictures of Mexico's Dia de los Muertos (Day of the Dead) celebrations to get an impression of this distinctive spiritual iconography.
- *The Tempest*: Deane also drew inspiration from a scene in William Shakespeare's play *The Tempest*, in which the character Ariel reflects on the change that occurs in death, in the song *Full Fathom Five Thy Father Lies*.

Full Fathom Five Thy Father Lies

Full fathom five thy father lies;

Of his bones are coral made;

Those are pearls that were his eyes:

Nothing of him that doth fade,

But doth suffer a **sea-change**

Into something rich and strange.

Sea-nymphs hourly ring his knell:

Ding-dong.

Hark! now I hear them,—ding-dong, bell.

From *The Tempest*, William Shakespeare

Deane dedicated the canon in *Seachanges* to the late American composer and resident of Mexico, Conlon Noncarrow, who was renowned for his complex canonic writing.

key point

A **canon** is where there is strict imitation between two or more melodic parts at a fixed distance (i.e. after a certain number of beats) and pitch (i.e. an interval of an octave, a third, etc.) apart.

Mexican Musical Influences in *Seachanges*

The use of ethnic percussion instruments, such as the maracas, marimba and guiro, gives a Mexican sound to the piece. These instruments originate in South America and are regularly used in Latin music.

Deane also instructs the violin and cello to strum at certain points of the work. This resembles the sound of the guitars in the Mexican folk music of the Mariachi bands.

Have your set works handy at all times. Put them onto your phone, your laptop or wherever you listen to music on a regular basis. It is vital that you are familiar with the set work to do well on the listening papers.

Features of Twentieth-Century Music in *Seachanges*

You should be able to understand and recognise 20th-century stylistic features and how Deane applies them to *Seachanges*.

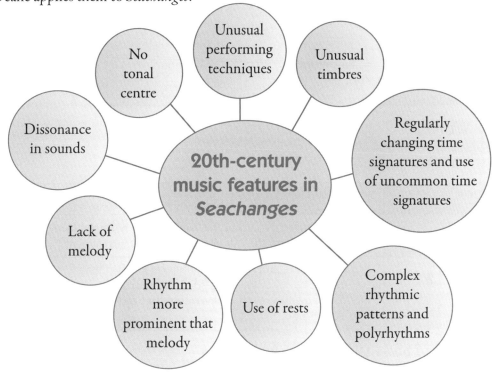

key point

A tonal centre gives music a sense of a 'home key' or a tonic note. Music without a tonal centre is **atonal**. It is difficult to define key, tonality or a clear melodic structure in atonal music.

> **Polyrhythms** occur when more that one type of rhythm is played at the same time and each rhythm contains a different pulse.

Instrumentation

Western Instruments	Western Percussion	Ethnic Percussion
Violin	Cymbals	Crotales
Cello	Gong	Maracas
Piano	Tambourine	Guiro
Flute in G	Bass drum	Marimba
		Rainstick

Key Words

Instruments

Crotales	Small, tuned hand cymbals.
Guiro	A Latin-American percussion instrument that is played by passing a wooden stick along the ridges of the wooden instrument.
Marimba	Like a xylophone, but more resonant and lower-pitched.
Rainstick	A long, hollow tube with grains inside that can be shaken or turned from side to side.

Performance and Instrumental Techniques

Quindicesima	15ma	Play two octaves higher.
Flageolet	flag.	Use of harmonics (also indicated by a circle over the note).
Pizzicato	pizz.	Pluck.
Pizzicato +	pizz. +	Pluck the string with the left hand.
'Bartok' pizzicato:		Slap the string.
Lesse vibrar	l.v.	Let vibrate.
Col legno battuto	col legno batt.	Hit the string with the wood of the bow.

Con ped.		Use the sustain pedal.
Sec/Senza ped.		Dry, no pedal.
Meno ped.		Less sustain pedal.
Sul ponticello	sul pont.	String players play close to or even on the bridge.
Strummed		Indicated to strum (like a guitar).
Ottava bassa	8ba	Play an octave lower than written.
Ottava	8va	Play an octave higher than written.
Sul tasto		Play near or over the fingerboard.
Senza vibrato		Without vibrato.
Molto vibrato		With a lot of vibrato.
Cymbal arco		The cymbal is played with a violin or cello bow.
Una corda	UC	Use the soft pedal on the piano.
Flz		Tongue flutter on the flute.
Modo ordinario	modo ord.	Play in the ordinary way.
Tremolo		Repeated, fast bowing on the same note.
Strum		String players strum strings like a guitar.
Glissando	gliss.	Slide from one given note to another given note.

Dynamics, Articulation and Other Musical Terms

Martellato		Hammered out, strongly accented.
Legatissimo	legatiss.	Very smoothly.
Fortississimo	fff	Extremely loud.
Sforzato	sfffz	Suddenly extremely loud.
Piu forte	piu f	Louder.
Non troppo		Not too much.
Trill	tr.	Play the note and the note above, alternating rapidly.

Compositional Techniques

The Basics

Technique	Definition
Inversion	A given melody is turned upside-down. The distance between the intervals remains the same.
Subtraction principle	A note is subtracted from a given melody after each playing of the melody.
Addition	A note is added to a given melody after each playing.
Diminution	The note values are shortened on a given melody.
Augmentation	The notes values are lengthened on a given melody.
Canon	The melody is strictly imitated by one or more parts at a fixed distance.
Retrograde	The melody is played backwards.

Compositional Techniques in *Seachanges*

Technique	How it is applied in *Seachanges*
Use of a melodic cell	A three-note cell (**G-A-C**) is central to *Seachanges*. The cell is altered and develops throughout the work (**permutation**).
Use of bar rests	Used, especially in the intro, to create a sense of drama and surprise.
Irregularity	The composer uses extremes in dynamics and pitch. He frequently changes the time signature and tempo, and clashes tonal sounds with atonal sounds. These techniques create a sense of order vs disorder in the work.
Inversion	The three-note cell (**G-A-C**) is inverted and is played as **G-F-D**. See **bar 21 on flute, and bar 27 on cello**.
Subtraction Principle	The main melody is played in a six-note phrase, then four, until only one note from the melody is played. See **bars 27–34 on violin**.
Addition	The melody starts with one note, then two, then three until it plays a seven-note melody. See **bars 128–140 on piano**.
Diminution	The note values of the main melody are shortened. See **bar 37 on crotales, and bar 121 on piccolo**.

Augmentation	The note values of the main melody are lengthened **on violin and its inversion on cello at bar 74.**
Canon	The **Dies Irae** is inverted and played in canon by the **marimba and the violin at bar 93.**
Retrograde	Played on **marimba** at the start of **bar 94.**

Rhythmic Features

Feature	Example in *Seachanges*
Metronome markings indicate tempo change	Bar 1: ♩ = c.80 Bar 46: ♩ = 120
Changing time signatures	Bars 1–21 (7/4, 4/4, 7/4, 3/4, 5/4, etc.)
The prominence of the Danse Macabre/ Totentanz rhythm	
Unusual time signatures	7/4, 5/4, 8/8, 10/8
Complex rhythm in flute	Bars 76–84
Polyrhythms	Bar 54

Form and Tonality

Seachanges has a number of recurring musical ideas that transform and develop throughout the work.

- The three main musical ideas are: **the three-note cell, Danse Macabre/Totentanz, and Dies Irae.**
- There is an intro and coda at the beginning and end of the work.
- The work is mostly **atonal**. However, there are some sections that can be described as having a **tonal centre**. For example, G may be described as the tonal centre in section A of the work.

Structure

Section		Bars	Tonal Centre
Intro	Introduction (three-note cell)	1–20	G
A1	Main melody and inversion	21–45	G
B	Danse Macabre/Totentanz	46–73	Atonal
A2	Main melody and inversion	74–91	D
C	Dies Irae	92–127	Atonal
A3	Main melody	128–140	E♭
Coda	Totentanz and Dies Irae	141–174	C, A

The Musical Ideas

Three-Note Cell

Raymond Deane took the idea of the three-note cell – **G, A, C** – from one of his earlier compositions, *The Seagull Dreams of its Shadow*. These three notes are the basis of the *Seachanges*.

The three-note cell or the **main musical motif** is heard at the very start of the work:

The three-note cell forms the theme called the **main melody**. This melody is also heard in its **inversion**:

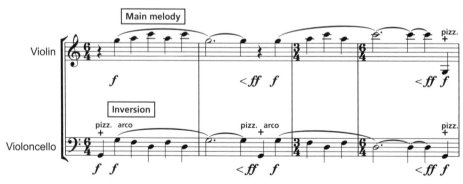

Danse Macabre/Totentanz

Dance-like rhythms associated with the Danse Macabre or 'Deathly Dance' are used to portray the theme of death.

Dies Irae

Deane uses part of the Dies Irae as the basis of the third theme. This piece is a well-known plainchant from the Roman Catholic Mass for the dead (or requiem). In Section C, the Dies Irae is played in canon by the marimba and violin (**distance of one bar and the same pitch**).

Analysis of *Seachanges* (with Danse Macabre)

Section		Bars	Points of interest
Introduction	Introduction (three-note cell)	1–8	G, A, C (three-note cell) played on crotales, piano, violin and piccolo
			Notes played at very high register
		1–16	Very light texture
		2, 10	Bars of silence
		7, 8, 10	Changes in time signature
		17	Descending chords on piano (inversion of G, A, C to G, F, D)
		17	A♭ note on piano
		17–20	Gong, maracas, bass drum and tambourine played in the introduction
			Cymbal played with bow
		19	Harmonics on cello and violin
		20	Violin played with the wood of the bow to give percussive sound

Section		Bars	Points of interest
Section A1	Main melody and inversion	21	Inversion of three-note cell (G, F, D) on cello in harmonics glissando of inversion on violin played on harmonics Subtraction principle applied to inversion on cello
		25	Ascending melody on marimba leads to main melody
		27	Main melody and inversion on violin and cello, with subtraction principle
		37	Diminution of main melody on crotales Main melody on marimba Inversion of main melody on piccolo
		38	♫♫ rhythm played on violin and cello with the wood of the bow
Section B	Danse Macabre/ Totentanz	46	Dance Macabre/Totentanz rhythm introduced
		49	Violin plays in parallel fifths
		50	Maracas and guiro are dominant
		51	Cello and violin strumming
		51	Violin plays across the bridge
		54	Martellato piano playing harsh dischords
		59	Piano and piccolo playing at extreme pitches
		60	*fff* dynamics towards end of section
		62/64	Bars of silence
		*Main melody and inversion heard **three times** in this section. All are subjected to the **subtraction principal**	
		65	*(1) Main melody and inversion on piano in diminution *fff* Repeated parallel fifths on violin and cello
		69–72	Totentanz rhythm on maracas, strummed cello and violin
Section A2	Main melody and inversion	74	*(2) Main melody and inversion on violin and cello in augmentation Much slower speed
		74–83	Cymbal, crotales and gong played
		76–85	Flute countermelody

Section		Bars	Points of interest
Section A2		77	Discords on piano
		85	Rainstick heard before third variant of main melody
			Ascending broken chords on piano (subtraction principal)
		86	Fluttering on flute
		88	*(3) Main melody and inversion on piano (LH = melody, RH = inversion)
Section C	Dies Irae	92	Tempo gets faster and repeated seconds played on violin (tremolo)
			Violin plays near bridge
		93	Dies Irae theme heard on marimba and played in canon, one bar later, on violin
		95	Piano player plays guiro
		99	Cello plays first phrase of Dies Irae in parallel fifths
		106	Piccolo play distorted phrase of Dies Irae with accents, at a very high register
			Cello plays second phrase of Dies Irae in fifths
		113	First and second phrase of Dies Irae played on piccolo, cello, marimba and violin. The melody is distorted and harsh sound is created by the use of dissonant intervals between cello and flute, and parallel fifths on strings (slides)
		115	Harsh *fff* clusters on piano
		117	March-like version of Dies Irae on piccolo, marimba and violin (staccato)
		121	Piccolo plays version of Dies Irae in diminution
		125	Use of rests and sparse texture at the end of this section
Section A	Main melody	128	Slower tempo and softer dynamics at beginning of section
			Duo for flute and piano based on main melody (augmentation)
			Subtraction on flute and addition on piano
			Danse Macabre rhythm played in triplets (G, A, C) on marimba
			E♭ note played on piano
		134	High pitched triplets played across the bridge on cello

Section	Bars	Points of interest
Coda	141	Faster tempo
		Very loud quavers on crotales at beginning of section
		C major chords in Danse Macabre/Totentanz rhythm played on violin and cello
	142	Chord clusters on marimba and piano
	144	Flute melody taken from canon at bar 93 (Dies Irae)
	150	C major stops at bar 150
		Fluttering on flute
		Chord clusters on marimba and piano
	155	Music builds to a climactic point with bass drum, cymbal and gong
	157	Totentanz rhythm played on guiro
	159	High B note is prominent on piccolo and marimba
	163	Marimba, piano and violin play note A in unison (cross rhythms)
		Chords played on piano based on the tritone
		Fifths played on violin and cello
		Played *fff*
	166	Note A on marimba, piano and violin
	172	Piano drops out, all other players take maracas

key point

A **tritone** is an interval of three tones between two given notes. In the Middle Ages, the tritone was known as '*diabolus in musica*' – 'the devil in music' – because of its dissonance.

exam TIPS

Read the question carefully. Are you asked to describe a feature heard in the **excerpt** or in the **overall work**?

Past Exam Questions

Year	Excerpt	Questions	Marks
2016 Q4 (10 marks)	Main Melody (A1)	(i) The theme heard in this excerpt is: (multiple choice).	1
		(ii) Name **three** percussion instruments playing in this excerpt.	1.5
		(iii) Describe **one** feature of the piano music in this excerpt.	1.5
		(iv) Name a compositional technique used in this excerpt.	1
		Describe how this technique is used in this excerpt.	2
		(v) How does this statement of the theme differ from the first time it is heard in *Seachanges with Danse Macabre*? Give **two** differences in your answer.	1.5+1.5
2015 Q1 (25 marks)	Excerpt 1: Introduction	(i) This excerpt is taken from the: (multiple choice).	1
		(ii) Insert the missing time signature in bar 5.	2
		(iii) In this excerpt the violin plays *flageolet* (*flag.*). Explain the term *flageolet*.	2
		(iv) Describe the use of a three-note cell in this excerpt.	3
	Excerpt 2: Main Melody and Inversion (A1)	(i) Name the theme heard in this excerpt.	2
		(ii) Which one of the following figures is heard in the accompaniment? (multiple choice).	2
		Name **one** instrument which plays this rhythm in this excerpt.	2
		(iii) Identify and describe a compositional technique used in this excerpt.	1+2
	Excerpt 3: Totentanz and Dies Irae (Coda)	(i) Describe the texture of the music heard in this excerpt.	3
		(ii) Describe **one** feature of the music played by the flute in this excerpt.	2
		(iii) Describe how Raymond Deane evokes the imagery of death in *Seachanges* with Danse Macabre.	3

exam TIPS

It is a good idea to go through the marking scheme and study the number of marks given to certain questions.

2014 Q4 (10 marks)	Dies Irae (C1)	(i) Identify the theme heard in this excerpt.	1
		(ii) Write down the order in which the instruments listed are heard at the start of the excerpt: violin, guiro, marimba.	2
		(iii) Name the compositional technique used in this excerpt. Describe how this technique is used in this excerpt.	1 / 2
		(iv) In this excerpt the cello plays *sul point*. Explain.	1
		(v) Describe some of the Mexican influences evident in *Seachanges with Danse Macabre*.	3
2010 Q1 (25 marks)	Excerpt 1: Introduction	(i) From which section of the work is this excerpt taken?	1
		(ii) Identify **three** percussion instruments heard playing in this excerpt. These instruments play: (multiple choice).	1×3 / 1
		(iii) The piccolo is first heard at: (multiple choice).	1
	Excerpt 2: Main Melody and Inversion (A1)	(i) Insert the **five** missing melody notes at **X** on the score.	1×5
		(ii) The instrumental technique below is heard in this excerpt. Describe this technique and identify the instrument(s) with which it is associated in this excerpt.	1+1
		(iii) Which if the following rhythmic figures can be heard in this excerpt? Describe one way in which this figure is used in the work.	1 / 2
	Excerpt 3: Main Melody and Inversion (A2)	(i) Identify and describe **two** compositional features/treatments of the melody heard in this excerpt.	2+2
		(ii) Describe **one** feature of the piano part in this excerpt.	2
		(iii) Outline the reasons for the composer's use of the word *Seachanges* in the title of this work.	3

The Beatles
Songs from Sgt. Pepper's Lonely Hearts Club Band

Sgt. Pepper's Lonely Hearts Club Band was the eighth studio album recorded by British band The Beatles, and was released in June 1967. It is regarded by many critics and musicians as one of the most influential albums of all time.

THE BAND

George Harrison	Lead guitar, vocals
John Lennon	Rhythm guitar, vocals
Paul McCartney	Bass guitar, vocals
Ringo Starr	Drums, vocals

Recording began on the album in 1966, when the 'Beatle mania' of the band's early years had begun to die down. The Beatles had received huge success in Europe and America, and in 1966 the band had decided to concentrate on recording new material rather than continuing their touring. They went to Abbey Road Studios, London, where they had access to the latest in recording technology and the assistance of their producer, George Martin.

The concept of the album was that the eponymous 'Sgt. Pepper's Lonely Hearts Club Band', with their outrageous costumes, long beards and moustaches, was the alter-ego of the Beatles. Many different styles and genres of music can be heard on the album, from the Indian sound of the sitar on *Within You, Without You*, to the jazz-inspired *When I'm Sixty-four*.

Sgt. Pepper's Lonely Hearts Club Band features many progressive arrangements for its time, mostly accredited to George Martin. Clarinets are featured on *When I'm Sixty-four*, a string nonet (nine instruments) and harp on *She's Leaving Home*, French horns on the title track, and a 40-piece orchestra for the final track *A Day in the Life*.

Key Words

Monosyllabic	Singing one note per syllable. This is a feature of the vocal line.
Contrapuntal or polyphonic texture	Two or more independent melodies played at the same time.
Plagal cadence	The Beatles used this finished IV–I cadence in many of their songs.

Flattened thirds and sevenths	The third and seventh notes in the major scale are lowered one semitone.
Syncopation	Emphasis on the rhythm is placed on the 'off' or 'weak' part of the beat.
Walking bass line	The bass guitar plays a bass line that moves by step. This is a common feature of jazz and blues music.
Modulation	Moving from one key to another key.
Triplets	Three notes played in the time of two notes of the same value.
Canon	Imitation between parts at a fixed distance and pitch.
Rondo form	The main theme recurs between different themes. For example, ABACAD, etc.
Slide	Sliding from one note to another note. This is an instrumental technique.
Vamping	Style of playing repeated chords heard on the piano in *When I'm Sixty-four*.
Dixieland jazz	Old jazz style that originated in New Orleans, Louisiana, USA in the early part of the 20th century. This style of jazz commonly has a wind instrument, such as a trumpet or clarinet, playing the melody, with piano and drums accompanying. The melody is highly syncopated and the bassline is steady and on-the-beat.
Word-painting	Music is used to enhance the lyrics and the story behind the song. For example, after the lyric 'she goes downstairs', the violins play a descending melodic pattern.
Art song	Form of classical song popular in 19th-century Europe.
Tremolo	Rapid bowing on a note, which produces a trembling effect.

Recording Techniques

Sgt. Pepper's Lonely Hearts Club Band is regarded as ground-breaking in terms of its production. A number of recording techniques and features that contribute to the unique sound of the music went on to inspire many other great artists.

Songs from *Sgt. Pepper's Lonely Hearts Club Band* are the only set works for which you need to demonstrate an understanding of how the **production** and engineering of the songs affects the music.

Be aware of how to explain the following techniques and also where they can be heard in each song.

Reverberation	An effect that adds an echo to the music.
Sampling	Taking a piece of sound from one recording and using it in a separate recording.
Double or multi-tracking	The layering of multiple recordings of sound. Each recording is connected to a track and eventually mixed together.
Distortion	An effect that makes the music sound 'overloaded'. It is a common effect used on guitars.

Side 1, Track 1: *Sgt. Pepper's Lonely Hearts Club Band*

Background to the Song

This is the opening track on the album. The concept of the song was conceived by Paul McCartney in November 1966, although its composition is credited to both John Lennon and McCartney. *Sgt. Pepper's Lonely Hearts Club Band* was recorded in Abbey Road Studios over a number of dates between 1 February and 6 March 1967. The song is preceded by the sound of an audience chattering and an orchestra tuning up; these were samples taken from a recording session of another song on the Sgt. Pepper album (*A Day in the Life*), and from recordings of *The Goon Show* in 1960. The song returns at a quicker tempo at the end of the album.

Instrumentation	Tonality	Metre	Style	Recording techniques	Texture
Vocals Lead guitar Rhythm guitar Bass guitar Drum kit French horn ×4	G major with modulation to F major in interlude sections	4/4	Rock/ pop with classical elements	Sampling Multi-tracking	**Homophonic** in verses **Polyphonic** in interludes **Two- and three-part vocal harmonies** in refrain

Analysis of Opening Track

Introduction: Bars 1–4

- The track fades up with the sound of an audience chatting and an orchestra tuning up.
- The song starts with drums, bass, and two guitars. The **opening chord** is A7 (V7 of V), resulting in tonal ambiguity.
- The four-bar chord structure is **A7, A7, C7, G7**.
- The **drum backbeat** sets up a rock and roll feel to the song. This is a **rhythmic feature** that can be found running through the song.

Backbeat rhythm is a common feature of rock music. It is a rhythm played on the drums where the bass drum is on the first and third beats with the hi-hat on the second and fourth beats.

Syncopation is where the emphasis is placed on the 'off' beat. It is a very common rhythmic feature of pop, rock, jazz and blues music.

When asked about style in the Beatles' music, remember that syncopation is a key feature of the melody in rock music. It is found in all three Beatles songs on the course.

Verse 1: Bars 5–12

- **Homophonic texture:** one main melody in vocals with guitar, bass and drums accompaniment.
- The melody of the first two phrases consists of a repeated tonic note (G) with the flattened seventh (F natural).
- Pay attention to the **syncopated rhythm** and the **chord structure** (G7, A7, C7, G7).

These chords have come up as a dictation exercise on the exam.

- The bass marks out the root of each chord with a **steady quaver beat**.
- The use of flattened **thirds and sevenths** adds a 'bluesy' sound to the melody.

Interlude 1: Bars 13–17

- Four French horns are added to the instrumentation at this point.
- Contrapuntal style on French horns creates a polyphonic texture.
- Modulation to F major.

Refrain: Bars 18–29

- Strong backbeat rhythm in drums and bass.
- Note values double from semiquavers in the verse to quavers in the refrain.
- Two- and three-part vocal harmonies.
- Rock sound on guitars.
- Flattened thirds and sevenths in vocals, as well as a syncopated rhythm.
- Unusual chord structure: G7, B♭7, C7, G7.
- Descending D7 arpeggio in horns.

Interlude 2: Bars 30–34

- The same chord structure as Interlude 1.
- Two- and three-part vocal harmonies (no vocals in Interlude 1).
- Sustained notes on the horns (bars 30–32).
- Contrapuntal texture on horns (bars 33–34).
- Descending walking bass line.

Verse 2: Bars 35–42

- Same music and structure as Verse 1, but different lyrics.
- More use of sampling in this section: the sound of a crowd clapping and cheering creates a sense of excitement.

Coda: Bars 43–45

- Sustained notes in horns (C7).
- Descending bass line.
- More audience sounds leading straight into next song on the album, *With a Little Help from My Friends*.

General Points of Interest in *Sgt. Pepper's Lonely Hearts Club Band*

The style of this song is pop/rock with classical elements:

- The pop/rock elements are the rock band, the use of flattened thirds and sevenths in the vocal lines, and the use of seventh chords.
- The classical elements are the use of the French horns and the contrapuntal texture in the interludes.

The C# and the F♮ create a modal sound. This feature can also be found in *She's Leaving Home*.

Recording techniques:

- Samples in the intro/coda
- Echo effects/reverberation in the vocals are used throughout the whole song

It is worth studying the **chord structure** of this song (see musical examples), as it has come up as harmonic dictation has been frequently asked in the questions relating to the Beatles' songs.

Melodic Features

- Repeated notes
- Monosyllabic melody
- Flattened thirds and sevenths

Rhythmic Features

- Syncopated rhythm in vocal line
- Steady backbeat in drums throughout
- Steady bass line punctuating chord changes and enhancing the 4/4 pulse

Harmonic Features

- Vocal harmonies in refrain and interlude 2

Side 2, Track 2: *When I'm Sixty-four*

Background to the Song

Paul McCartney wrote this song when he was 16 years old. The Beatles used it as a backup acoustic song if there were electrical problems during their early days on the road. George Martin stated that McCartney chose the song for the *Sgt. Pepper* album as his father turned 64 in 1966 – the year that the album was recorded. The song is about a young man talking to his lover about growing old together. This song was not one of the most popular songs amongst Beatles fans at the time of its release, although it did appeal to the band's older fans.

Instrumentation	Tonality	Metre	Style	Recording techniques	Texture
Piano Clarinet ×2 Bass clarinet Rhythm guitar Bass guitar Snare drum Chimes	C major	2/2	Pop/jazz/classical	Recording **sped up** to make McCartney's voice sound higher and therefore younger (D♭ major) **Double tracking** on vocal harmonies.	Polyphonic. Imitation between clarinets.

Section	Key Centre
Introduction	C
Verse 1 A B	C
Bridge 1 C D	A minor
Verse 2 A B	C
Bridge 2 C D	A minor
Verse 3 A B	C
Outro	C

exam TIPS

Note the changes from major to minor between the verses and bridges.

Analysis of *When I'm Sixty-four*

Introduction: Bars 1–6

- Clarinets play the opening syncopated melody in **imitation** (canonic entry).
- The bass clarinet keeps a steady beat.
- This opening is a jazz known as **ragtime** (listen to Scott Joplin's *Maple Leaf Rag*).

Clarinet

Verse 1: Bars 7–22

- Triadic and chromatic movement in the vocal line.
- The melody throughout the verse is **syncopated**.
- The bass keeps a steady beat throughout and the clarinets alternate between sustained notes and short **riffs** in between phrases (feature of Dixieland jazz).
- **Piano vamping** in second phrase (bar 11).
- At the end of the verse the clarinets mark the chord progressions in crochets, followed by triplets on bass clarinet, leading into the bridge section.

Bridge 1: Bars 23–39

- The music shifts to **A minor**, the melody moves away from the syncopated rhythm of the verse.
- **Clarinets play in descending thirds** along with **block chords on the piano** in the first bar of the bridge (bar 23).
- There are two and three part vocal harmonies in the first phrase (bars 23–30) of the bridge.
- 'Jazzy' slide on the clarinet leads into the **D phrase**.
- Alberti bass on the piano in the **D phrase**.
- The **chimes** and the **hi-hat** can also be heard at the end of this section, as the music shifts from A minor back to C major.

Verse 2: Bars 40–55

Verse 2 is almost the same as verse 1. There are subtle changes in the clarinets.

Bridge 2: Bars 56–72

- The vocals are heard from the beginning of this section.
- The harmonic structure is the same as bridge 1.
- Backing vocals echoing *'we shall scrimp and save'* at bar 61.
- The hi-hat is more prominent in the second half of this bridge.
- The chimes play a more syncopated melody than heard in the first bridge.

Verse 3: Bars 89–92

- This verse is also very similar to verse 1. However, there are significant instrumental differences.
- At the start of the verse, the clarinet plays in **sixths**, and then **thirds**, against the vocal line. The rhythm guitar is heard for the first time.
- The guitar and clarinets emphasise the jazz aspects of this song.
- Paul McCartney expresses the light-hearted nature of the song in his vocals, especially in the last phrase of this verse.

Outro/Coda: Bars 89–92

- The clarinet line from the introduction is heard once more to close the song.
- The song finishes with a **perfect cadence**.

General Points of Interest in *When I'm Sixty-four*

- The **style** of this song is jazz/pop/classical:
  - The jazz elements are the use of the clarinets, the ragtime idioms throughout the song, the syncopated nature of the melody, chord structure and performance techniques such as **slides** on the clarinets.
  - The pop element is Paul McCartney's vocal style.
  - The classical elements are the canonic entries in clarinets (intro), and its similarities with the classical rondo form.
- The key centre is C major, but there is a change in tonality (A minor) in the bridge sections.
- There are homophonic to polyphonic changes in texture between the verses and bridges.
- There is a change in the melody in Bridge 1; it has slower note values and moves away from the syncopated melody of Verse 1.
- Vocals enter from the start of Bridge 2, which is not the case in Bridge 1.
- Note also the differences between Verses 1 and 2, and Verse 3: there are changes in the clarinet parts, and the guitar is added to Verse 3 (not in Verses 1 and 2).

Performance techniques	Vamping on the piano
	Slides on the clarinets
Compositional features	Canonic writing in the intro
	Alberti bass in the piano accompaniment in the bridge section

Side 1, Track 6: *She's Leaving Home*

Background to the song

This song was written by Lennon and McCartney in 1967. McCartney was inspired to write the song when he read an article about a young girl who had left home. In the song, McCartney describes the events of the girl leaving and the worry and sorrow felt by her parents. This is one of a few songs on which the band does not play.

She's Leaving Home was arranged by Mike Leander. The band's producer and arranger, George Martin, was unavailable to arrange this track, although he did produce it. Lennon's part in the song is that of the parent's feelings in the chorus: '*What did we do that was wrong*'.

Instrumentation
Vocals
String nonet: violins ×4, violas ×2, cellos ×2, double bass
Harp

Tonality	Metre	Style	Recording techniques	Texture
E major (written in piano/ vocal edition in E♭ major)	3/4	Pop ballad with classical elements	Double tracking Echo effects	Homophonic in verses Contrapuntal texture in choruses

Section	Bar	Form
Introduction	1–4	
Verse 1	5–36	ABAB
Chorus	37–55	CD
Verse 2	56–87	ABAB
Chorus 2	88–106	CD
Verse 3	107–122	AB
Chorus 3	123–142	CD
Coda	143–150	E

Introduction: Bars 1–4

- Harp arpeggios in E major with an added C♯ and A.
- Block chords on lower end of harp.
- This musical idea returns at the end of the song.

Verse 1: Bars 5–36

A

Melody: Syncopated rhythm and flattened seventh in bar 7.

Accompaniment: Quavers on harp.

Link: Ascending cello solo. Note the raised fourth.

B

Melody: '*Silently closing ...*' Two four-bar vocal phrases.

Accompaniment: Sustained B7 chords on cello, viola and violins.

A

Melody: Repeat of Section A.

Accompaniment: Harp quaver chords joined by long notes on cello.

Link: Two-part counterpoint between violin and cello. Parts move in contrary motion.

B

Repeat of Section B.

Chorus 1: Bars 37–55

C

- Two-part vocal harmony over a sustained E major chord.
- 12-bar phrase.

exam TIPS

Note the descending scale and the words '*she goes downstairs*'. This is an example of **word-painting**.

D

- Irregular seven-bar phrase.
- Abrupt ending (chords on strings).

Verse 2: Bars 56–87

A

Melody: Repeat of Verse 1.

Accompaniment: Strings provide the accompaniment; triadic movement in cello and double bass ('stabbing chords') while high strings play long notes in thirds.

B

Melody: Repeat of Verse 1.

Accompaniment: Similar to Verse 1.

A

Melody: *'She breaks down'* is followed by three-bar link of **syncopated triplets** on violins illustrating the mother's weeping.

Note: this is the only set of triplets in this song.

B

Melody: Repeat of Section B.

Accompaniment: Descending scale on harp leading into Chorus 2.

Chorus 2: Bars 88–106

- Similar to the first chorus.
- Some changes in the strings.
- Lower strings play arpeggios of E major (heard in the harp intro).

Verse 3: Bars 107–122

This verse is **16 bars shorter** than verses 1 and 2.

A

Melody: Similar to previous A phrases.

Accompaniment:

- 'Stabbing chords' now in **harp and upper strings.**
- A **three-part counterpoint on strings** at the end of this phrase.

B

Melody: Similar to previous B phrases.

Accompaniment:

- **Tremolo in violins** used to enhance the anxiety expressed in the lyrics.
- **Disjointed quavers** played on cello to represent the sound of the engines: *'meeting a man from the motor trade'*.

Chorus 3: Bars 123–142

C

Melody: Similar to chorus 2.

Accompaniment: Violins play at a higher pitch and sounding more agitated.

D

Melody: An additional eight bars to the D section.

Coda: Bars 143–149

Melody: Long notes in vocals.

Accompaniment: Strings and harp.

The song ends with a **plagal cadence (IV–I)**. The harp echoes the arpeggios from the introduction for the last three bars.

General Points of Interest in *She's Leaving Home*

The style of this song is a fusion of pop ballad and classical.

- The pop/ballad elements are the use of the raised fourth and flattened seventh notes (**mixolydian**, a mode is used in popular music), along with the vocal style.
- The classical elements to this song are evident in the instrumentation, i.e. the string arrangement. It is also similar in style to 19th-century art song, which used music to enhance the mood of a song and to strengthen the meaning of the lyrics.

Harmony:

- The use of the chord of F♯ major is prominent in *She's Leaving Home* and is also found in *Sgt. Pepper* and *When I'm Sixty-four*.

Rhythmic features:

- **Syncopation** in the vocal and string lines
- **Triplets** in bars 76 and 77 in the violins

Word-painting in *She's Leaving Home*

Verse	Lyrics Reference	Technique
1	*'She goes downstairs'*	Descending step movement on the violins.
2	*'She breaks down and cries to her husband'*	Triplets and repeated notes on the violin to suggest weeping.
3	*'Waiting to keep the appointment she made'*	Tremolos on the violins suggest excitement.
3	*'Meeting a man from the motor trade'*	Disjointed quavers in the lower strings suggest the sound of the engines.

Musical Style of Songs from *Sgt. Pepper's Lonely Hearts Club Band*

In the exam, students are commonly asked to discuss the style of the songs. Be careful to **refer to the music or musical features** in your answer.

Here is a sample answer when asked to discuss the style of the three songs. There are many possible correct answer, but you will likely only need to give two or three relevant points in the exam.

SAMPLE EXAM QUESTION

Sgt. Pepper's Lonely Hearts Club Band

- Rock/pop with classical elements
- Use of the rock band medium
- Standard back beat on the drums
- Syncopation and flattened thirds and sevenths in the melody
- Use of French horns for classical sound
- Contrapuntal texture is a feature commonly heard in classical music

When I'm Sixty-four

- Pop with jazz elements
- Pop style of singing
- Brushes often used on drums in jazz music
- Vamping chords on the piano is a feature common to jazz
- Swing style of playing on the clarinet
- Use of flattened notes common to pop and jazz
- Slides heard on the clarinet is a common feature of jazz

She's Leaving Home

- Pop ballad with classical elements
- Pop style of singing
- Use of string nonet and harp is classical
- Similar in style to an art song
- Use of word-painting is a common feature of Western art song (e.g. the violin plays descending step movement after the lyric 'She goes downstairs', highlighting the movement of going down stairs)
- Use of the plagal cadence at the end of the song, which is more common to classical music.

Past Exam Questions

Year	Song	Questions	Marks
2021 Q4 (10 marks)	*She's Leaving Home*	(a) Describe **one** feature of the introduction.	2
		(b) Describe **one** feature of the vocal music in this excerpt.	2
		(c) The rhythm played by the strings at the end of line 2 and line 3 is: (multiple choice).	2
		(d) A feature of the accompaniment at the end of line 4 is: (multiple choice).	2
		(e) This song contains examples of picture painting. Describe one example of picture painting in the music heard in this excerpt.	2

In the 2021 listening paper, the exam questions used the term **picture painting** for the first time. This is the same as **word-painting**.

2016 Q3 (10 marks)	When I'm Sixty-four	(a) Name the woodwind instrument heard in lines 1–3 of this excerpt. Describe what it plays.	1 2
		(b) The bass line rhythm heard in lines 4–5 is: (multiple choice).	2
		(c) Identify **two** features of the vocal part as heard in this excerpt.	1+1
		(d) Identify the style of this song.	1
		(e) Describe **two** differences between the music of this verse and the music of verse 1 in When I'm Sixty-four.	1+1
2015 Q4 (10 marks)	Sgt. Pepper's Lonely Hearts Club Band	(i) Which of the following rhythms is heard in the vocal part of line 1: (multiple choice).	1
		(ii) The chord for the underlined word in line 2 is: (multiple choice).	1
		(iii) The accompaniment in lines 1–4 features: (multiple choice).	1
		(iv) Identify **two** features (melodic and/or rhythmic) of the melody in lines 1–7 of this excerpt.	1.5+1.5
		(v) Name the instruments which enter after line 7. Identify **two** features of the music played by these instruments.	1 1.5+1.5

Year	Song	Questions	Marks
2014 Q2 (10 marks)	When I'm Sixty-four	(i) How many bars of music are heard in the introduction?	1
		Identify **three** instruments that play in the introduction	1.5
		(ii) Identify **two** features of the vocal line heard in lines 1 and 2 of this excerpt.	1+1
		(iii) Which rhythm can be heard in the accompaniment in line 3: (multiple choice).	1
		(iv) Describe the texture of the music heard in lines 5–6.	2
		(v) Identify and describe the style of When I'm Sixty-four.	0.5+2
2010 Q4 (10 marks)	She's Leaving Home	(i) Identify the time signature of the music in this excerpt.	1
		(ii) Briefly describe the music played by the strings immediately after line 1.	2
		(iii) Which **three** of the following features can be heard in the music in lines 2–3: (multiple choice).	1+1+1
		(iv) Describe the vocal texture of lines 4–7.	2
		(v) Identify the last **two** notes of the vocal line: (multiple choice).	1
		Identify the cadence at the end of the excerpt.	1

2 Irish Music

By the end of this chapter, you will be able to:

- understand what you need to study to answer a question on Irish music
- describe key elements of traditional Irish music
- explain the differences between the different types of Irish dances
- understand how to frame a strong essay question

The Irish music question is worth 25 marks.

The question is divided into two parts:

- a listening section worth 15 marks
- an essay question worth 10 marks

Listening Section (15 marks)

The listening section of the exam usually consists of **three** excerpts of music. These excerpts test your knowledge on the following traditional Irish music elements:

Dances	Identify the dance
	Bar(s) of rhythm
	Time signature
	Form
Songs	Identify the song type
	List typical features of the song type
	Form
Instruments	Identify melodic instruments
	Identify harmonic and rhythmic instruments
Traditional ('trad') and non-trad features	Identify trad features
	Identify non-trad features
Style/Fusion	Identify the style of the given excerpt and refer to the particular features of that style

Instruments used in Traditional Irish Music

Melody	Harmony	Rhythm
Fiddle	Harp	Bodhrán
Flute	Guitar	Bones and spoons
Uilleann pipes	Bouzouki	Drum kit
Harp	Piano/keyboard	Variety of percussion
Banjo (since approx. 1900)		
Tin whistle		
Accordion		
Concertina		

Irish Dance Music

Dance music is the most common form of Irish music. Most Irish dance tunes date back to the 18th and 19th centuries, and were often influenced by other European dances.

- Irish dance tunes usually have two sections (A and B) consisting of eight bars each.
- Both sections are repeated in the form AABB.
- The 'A' section is known as the 'tune', while the 'B section' is called the 'turn'.
- Section B usually has a higher range of notes than the Section A.
- A 'set' is when one dance runs into another dance.

Dance	Time signature	Bar of rhythm	Features	Examples
Double jig	6/8		Nearly all quaver movement Lively tempo	*Connachtman's Rambles* *Saddle the Pony*
Single jig	6/8		Crotchet, quaver movement Lively tempo	*Haste to the Wedding*
Slip/ Hop jig	9/8		Metre of three Lively tempo	*Drops of Brandy* *The Butterfly*
Reel	4/4 time		Lively tempo Most popular dance form	*Drowsy Maggie* *The Maid behind the Bar*
Hornpipe	4/4 time		Not as lively as a reel Dotted rhythm Accent on first and third beats	*Off to California* *Harvest Home*
Polka	2/4 time		Lively tempo	*Britches Full of Stitches* *Kerry Polka*
Slide	12/8 time		Faster than single jig Popular in Cork/ Kerry region	*Merrily Kissed the Quaker*

Fusion

Irish traditional music mixed with other styles and genres is known as **fusion**.

Title	Performers	Style	Trad features	Non-trad features
The Lobster	The Gloaming	Traditional + Celtic/ Classical	Ornamentation Dance rhythm Steady dance (reel) pulse	Piano accompaniment Unusual harmonies Changes in tonality Countermelodies

Title	Performers	Style	Trad features	Non-trad features
Drowsy Maggie	Matt Molloy	Traditional + Folk	Reel Ornamentation Starts solo melody Steady reel pulse	Guitar chords Countermelody on flute
The Butterfly	Myrddin Quartet	Traditional + Celtic/Folk	Ornamentation Slip jig rhythm	Non-trad instruments (guitars/mandolin/cello)
Glanfaidh Mé	Kila	Traditional + Rock/Ethnic/World	Reel rhythm Ornamentation Use of trad instruments	Non-trad instruments (drums, electric and bass guitar, ethnic drums) Harmonic accompaniment Vocal harmonies
Oíche Nollaig	Mícheál Ó Súilleabháin	Traditional + Jazz/Classical	Reel rhythm Ornamentation Strict rhythm	Harmonic accompaniment Syncopation Use of seventh chords Contrasts in dynamics
Toss the Feathers	The Corrs	Traditional + Rock	Ornamentation Reel Strict time Dance structure Tin whistle and fiddle	Non-trad instruments (drums, electric and bass guitar) Syncopation in accompaniment Guitar power chords Drum solo and fills

Irish Song

Features of Sean Nós Singing

Sean nós is a form of traditional Irish singing. It is unaccompanied and has a simple form, with free rhythm and a wide range in melody. Ornamentation and slides are commonly used to embellish the rhythm and melody, but there are few or no changes in dynamics. A modal or gapped scale is used, and the last note is usually repeated. Different regions of Ireland have different styles of sean nós.

Regional Styles in Sean Nós

Region	Features	Performer	Notable Performance
Donegal	Some nasal style Some ornamentation Influenced by Scots-Gaelic singing More regular rhythm	Lillis Ó Laoire	*The Congregation on Sunday* from 'Celtic Mouth Music'
Connemara	Lot of ornamentation Nasal tone quality	Róisín Elsafty Seosamh Ó hÉanaí	*Eleanóir na Rún* ('Sean Nós Singing' 2:36, clarebannerman) ▶ YouTube
Munster	Some vibrato used Wide range in melody Lots of ornamentation	Iarla Ó Lionáird	*Casadh an tSúgáin* from 'Brooklyn' Original Soundtrack

Irish Folk Songs, Ballads and Anglo-Irish Songs

Irish folk songs sung in the English language have been passed down from generation to generation. The songs are generally about social issues or historical events. Regional accents can be heard in many Irish folk songs.

Instruments such as guitar, fiddle, tin whistle, bouzouki and mandolin are regularly used in Irish folk music. The music of each verse is generally the same.

As a result of emigration, many Irish folk songs became very influential in North America in the 19th century.

The songs of Thomas Moore became popular in the 19th century. They generally have a piano accompaniment and are classical in style.

Bands such as The Dubliners, The Clancy Brothers and Planxty brought a new popularity to Irish folk music in the 1960s and 1970s. Popular artists such as Damien Dempsey, Seán Keane and Declan O'Rourke keep the folk tradition alive today.

Recommended Listening

Artist(s)	Song	Features
The Clancy Brothers	*The Parting Glass* (1959)	AABA form Simple guitar chord accompaniment

Artist(s)	Song	Features
The Dubliners	*Dirty Old Town* (1968)	Fiddle and tin whistle doubling the melody Chordal accompaniment on banjo and guitars Regional accent in vocals
Luke Kelly	*Raglan Road* (1983)	AABA form Historical ballad Ornamentation Banjo accompaniment Free rhythm Fiddle and tin whistle doubling the melody
The Pogues	*Rainy Night in Soho* (1985)	Ornamentation Strophic form Regional accent in vocals Guitar Use of trad instruments such as fiddle and mandolin
Mary Black	*Bright Blue Rose* (1991)	Guitar and accordion accompaniment Modern Irish ballad Vocal harmonies in chorus American 'blues' influence on guitar
Sinéad O'Connor and The Chieftains	*The Foggy Dew* (1995)	AABA form Historical ballad Ornamentation Wide range in melody Trad instruments such as fiddle, tin whistle, bodhrán
The Fureys	*When You Were Sweet Sixteen* (1999)	Modern Irish ballad Classical elements such as use of strings and cello countermelody Slow tempo

Essay Section (10 marks)

Although this is a written section, it is important to give evidence of listening in your answer. There is a choice of four topics and you must answer one.

Recently Examined Essay Topics

Discuss or give an account of within the context of Irish traditional music:	Year Examined
A well-known group/band/composer that fuses Irish traditional music with another style of music	2021
The role of the collector in Irish traditional music	2021
Regional styles in Irish traditional music	2021
Sean nós singing in the Irish language	2020
Use of fusion	2020
Developments in Irish music in the 20th century	2019
Ornamentation in instrumental music	2019, 2016
Dance music	2019, 2016, 2013
Uillean pipes	2019
Irish song tradition	2018, 2016, 2012
Changes in Irish music in the 20th century, with reference to regional styles	2018
Group/band that fuses Irish traditional music with another style	2018
19th-century collectors and their contribution to the preservation of Irish traditional music	2018
The Uilleann pipes or the Irish harp	2017
Musical style of any well-known group	2017
The Céilí band tradition	2020, 2017, 2014
The contribution of Irish music to the folk music of North America	2021, 2017, 2015, 2014
Seán Ó Riada	2016
Preservation of Irish music from 20th century onwards	2015
Regional styles in instrumental music	2015
The harping tradition	2021, 2020, 2015, 2013

- Keep a note/log of performers and recordings that you have listened to during your studies, research and revision of Irish music.
- Remember that this is a written question on the **listening paper,** so your answer must be supported by evidence of listening.
- Demonstrate evidence of listening by providing relevant musical examples in your essay such as publications, recordings, concert performances, online resources, etc.
- Give clear and concise statements in your chosen essay. You only have approximately 10 minutes for this question, so make sure every sentence is relevant to the topic.

The Céilí Band Tradition

A céilí band is a group of approximately eight to ten musicians gathered for the purpose of providing music for dance.

The first céilí band is believed to have been formed in London in 1897. Radio broadcasts helped the promotion of céilí band music from the 1930s and 1940s, when the Public Dance Halls Act prohibited dances in unauthorised establishments. Dances were usually held in (authorised) parish halls.

Instruments typically used for melody are fiddles, flutes, and button accordions. These instruments usually play in unison. A snare drum is commonly used to provide the strict dance rhythm needed for dancing, while a piano is used to provide a bass and chordal accompaniment by means of vamping.

Other instruments sometimes used in céilí bands are harmonicas, uilleann pipes, banjos and saxophones.

The Fleadh Cheoil, an annual traditional Irish music festival, has had a major impact on the promotion and popularity of the Céilí Band tradition.

Vamping is a way of playing a pattern of chords over and over. Piano vamping adds to the harmony and pulse of the music.

Notable bands include the Kilfenora and Tulla Céilí Bands.

Artist(s)	Song	Features
Kilfenora Céilí Band	*Molly Bán* (Reel set) (2019)	Traditional line-up of fiddles, flutes, button accordion, banjo, drums and piano Steady pulse
Blackwater Céilí Band	*CCÉn Gleann An Chlochair, Tir Eoghan* (2:21, FleadhTV) ▶ YouTube	Flutes, fiddles, button accordion, drums and keyboard Steady pulse

Mícheál Ó Súilleabháin

Born in Clonmel, 1950, Mícheál Ó Súilleabháin was Emeritus Professor of Music at the University of Limerick, and the founder and director of the Irish World Academy of Music and Dance.

After studying at University College Cork with the composers Aloys Fleischmann and Seán Ó Riada, and later at Queens University College in Belfast, Ó Súilleabháin became a renowned composer, educator and broadcaster of Irish music. He was particularly respected for his development of a uniquely Irish traditional piano style and his fusion of harp tunes, Irish airs and dance tunes with classical, jazz and contemporary genres. He recorded extensively with the Irish Chamber Orchestra.

Song	Where to Find It	Features
Oíche Nollaig	Album: The Dolphin's Way (1987)	Piano piece, combines classical piano style with Irish trad (dance rhythms, bodhrán, bones, ornamentation) and jazz elements such as syncopated rhythms, blues notes and a jazz 'break' on piano.
Woodbrook	Album: Between Worlds (1995)	Irish air played on piano with a string orchestra Fusion of trad and classical style
Medley of Woodbrook, Oíche Nollaig and the Old Grey Goose	'Mícheál Ó Súilleabháin and the RTÉ Concert Orchestra performance at IFTA 2011' (6:17, IFTAAwards) ▶ YouTube	Fusion of trad, classical and jazz

The Harping Tradition

The harper held an important position in the household of the great nobles of the Middle Ages. Tunes that the harpers composed for their patrons were called 'planxties'. The harps had wire strings that were played with long fingernails. The oldest surviving harp from this period is the Brian Boru harp, which is on display at the Trinity College library.

Throughout the 16th and 17th centuries, the harp went into decline due to the plantations and penal laws. Many harps were destroyed during these years. Three men – Dr James McDonnell, Robert Bradshaw and Henry Joy – organised the Belfast Harp Festival in 1792 in order to preserve and promote the dying art. They hired a young musician called Edward Bunting to notate (write down) some of the tunes played by the harpers. In 1796, Bunting published *The Ancient Music of Ireland*, which contained the tunes that he had notated at the Belfast Harp Festival, and helped to establish the harp as a symbol of Irish national identity.

Now, the harping tradition is maintained by Cairde na Cruite, an organisation established in 1960 to promote the harp, publish harp music and contribute to the role of the harp in Irish traditional music.

The International Irish Harp Festival is held in Termonfeckin, Co. Louth every year. This event attracts visitors and musicians from all over the world.

Artist(s)	Song	Album
Máire Ní Chathasaigh	*The Humours of Ballyloughlin*	The New Strung Harp (1985)
Laoise Kelly	*Carolan's Farewell to Music*	Just Harp (1999)

Regional Styles in Fiddle Playing

There are three main regional styles of fiddle playing: Donegal, Sligo and Clare. These styles can be classified by their use of:

- Phrasing
- Ornamentation
- Articulation
- Bowing
- Variation
- Tempo

Region	Player	Features	Listen to
Donegal	Mairéad Ní Mhoanaigh	Short bows Staccato style bowing One note per bow Double stopping Some ornamentation Fast tempo	The Lancers The Further in the Deeper (Jigs)
Sligo	Michael Coleman	Smooth bowing Use of rolls and turns Highly ornamented Fast tempo	The Pigeon on the Gate
Clare	Martin Hayes	Smooth rhythmic bowing Use of triplets, rolls and slides Delicate style of playing Sweet tone	The Sailor's Bonnet

Collectors

As Irish music is generally an oral tradition, the survival of Irish music was dependent on memory. The work of music 'collectors' played a pivotal role in the preservation of Irish music. Without them, many songs, airs and dance tunes would have died out.

Today, recording and preservation of music is much more accessible, but contemporary collectors still play a vital role in the preservation of a musical heritage.

Captain Francis O'Neill (1848–1936)

- Arguably the most important collector of Irish dance music.
- Alongside Irish musician, and co-member of the police force in Chicago, James O'Neill, he collected, notated and preserved the tunes of musicians based in Chicago in the latter part of the 19th century.
- Published The Music of Ireland, a collection of 1,850 tunes (1903).
- Published The Dance Music of Ireland, which contained 1,001 tunes (1907). This is commonly referred to as 'The Book'.
- Collected some of the tunes from the famous piper, Patsy Touhy.
- **Notable piece:** The Tenpenny Bit by Dervish

Edward Bunting (1773–1843)

- Employed to notate the music of the harpers at the Belfast Harp Festival in 1792.
- After the Harp Festival, he travelled around Ireland collecting songs and tunes.

- He published three volumes of music: *The Ancient Music of Ireland Vols I, II and III* (1796, 1809 and 1840).
- **Notable piece:** *Casadh an tSugain* by Iarla Ó Lionáird

George Petrie (1790–1866)

- Born in Dublin.
- His collection *Ancient Music of Ireland* was published in 1855. This collection of 147 airs contains detailed notes on the tunes.
- *The Londonderry Air*, also known as *Danny Boy*, is part of this collection. Petrie obtained it from Miss Jane Ross of Limavady.
- **Notable piece:** *The Blackberry Blossom* by Planxty

The Influence of Irish Music on the Music of North America

Many Irish people emigrated to North America and Canada during the 18th and 19th centuries, bringing with them their vast repertoire of songs, airs and dance music. Irish song and dance music merged with music from other cultures in the 'melting pot' of North America.

Following the invention of the gramophone in 1887, many Irish musicians were recorded in America in the early part of the 20th century. Michael Coleman, a Sligo-born fiddler, was recorded during the 1920s and his regional style influenced generations of fiddlers throughout America and Ireland.

Examples of Irish music in North America:

- The folk music of the Appalachian Mountains area was given the name 'The High Lonesome Sound'. It was heavily influenced by the melodies, structure and style of Irish music.
- The song *Rose Connolly*, originally collected by Edward Bunting, became popular in America and was recorded by The Everly Brothers.
- The American ballad *The Streets of Laredo* by Johnny Cash has the same melody as the Irish ballad *Bard of Armagh*.

Artist(s)	Song	Features
The Charlie Daniels Band	*The Devil Went down to Georgia* (1979)	Bluegrass fused with country rock style. The fiddle playing is heavily influenced by bluegrass/ Appalachian style
Alison Krauss and Gillian Welch	*I'll Fly Away* (2000)	A popular bluegrass song that has its roots in gospel music

Michael Coleman	*The Tarbolton Reel* (1934)	Recorded in America Demonstrates Coleman's fast and heavily ornamented style of fiddle playing
Johnny Cash	*The Streets of Laredo* (1965)	American ballad that has the same tune as the Irish ballad *Bard of Armagh*

Leaving Certificate Examination 2018, Question 5

Section A

Excerpt	Question	Answer	Marks
Excerpt 1: Patsy Ó Ceannabháin *Fear Múinte Mánla, An Bonnán Buí* (5 marks)	(i) Identify the style of singing in this excerpt.	Sean nós	1
	(ii) Identify **three** features of this style of singing, as heard in this excerpt.	Sung solo; unaccompanied; sung with ornamentation; na-sal tone; sung with free rhythm (didn't accept 'sung in Irish' or 'wide range')	1+1+1
	(iii) Identify the form of the verse (multiple choice).	AABA	1
Excerpt 2: The Chieftains, *Carolan's Concerto* (4 marks)	(i) Identify three different instruments playing the melody in this excerpt.	Harp(s); uileann pipes; tin whistle; flute; fiddle	0.5+0.5 +0.5
	(ii) Identify the feature of trad music heard in this excerpt.	Repeated last note	0.5
	(iii) *Carolan's Concerto* is often described as being Baroque in style. Identify **two** features of the music heard in this excerpt which support this statement.	Use of sequences; cadences; (terraced) dynamics; very structured; reference to texture; ornamentation; homophonic; strict rhythm/tempo	1+1

Excerpt	Question	Answer	Marks
Excerpt 3: The Chieftains, *Lots of Drops of Brandy* (6 marks)	This excerpt consists of three different dances based on the tune *Drops of Brandy*. In the case of each one, identify the type of dance and give its time signature and one bar of rhythm associated with it.	Dance 1: (single/double) jig; 6/8 Dance 2: reel; 4/4 or 2/2 or 2/4 Dance 3: slip/hop jig; 9/8	1+0.5+0.5 1+0.5+0.5 1+0.5+0.5

Marking Scheme

Up to 10 marks for quality of answers and knowledge of topic chosen.		
Excellent awareness and detailed knowledge of musical features of topic.	10	
Very good knowledge of musical features of chosen topic.	8–9	
Good knowledge of topic, but lacking in detail.	6–7	
Some general points on topic, but lacking sufficient detail.	4–5	10
Generally inadequate response to chosen topic.	2–3	
Little response to chosen topic in evidence.	1	
No response to chosen topic in evidence.	0	

Clarifications:
(i) Accept any aspect of songs or sean-nós or a combination of both.
(ii) Answers must refer to a group/band (i.e. not a composer or solo performer).

3 Aural Skills

By the end of this chapter you will be able to:

- understand and identify all key musical features that may be examined in Question 6 of the exam
- apply your knowledge and study of the set works
- identify and understand a range of musical genres and performance mediums

General Information

Question 6 on the Listening Paper is worth 20 marks.

This question examines your musical awareness and ability to identify and describe musical features in a piece that you may not have heard before.

The music played in this question can be from any style or genre, e.g. pop/rock, jazz, classical, folk, ethnic. The music may be instrumental, vocal, choral or a combination of these.

There may be two or three sections in this question. Each section is usually played three times.

You may be asked to compare an unheard piece with the style of one of your set works.

Preparing for the Examination

When preparing for Question 6 of the examination you should:

- Develop a good understanding of your set works. What you have studied for the set works questions may be relevant for Question 6. The set works are analysed using the topics in the mind map on the next page. Features relating to these topics should also be studied for Question 6.

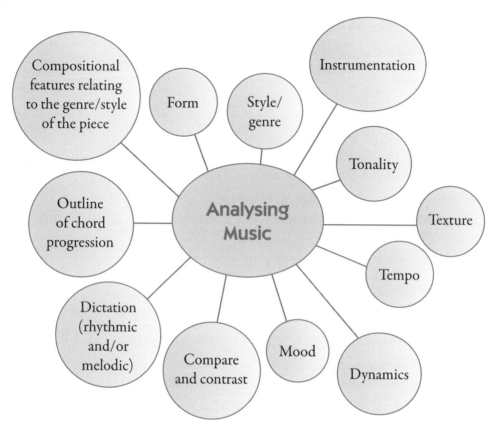

- Listen to a wide variety of musical styles.
- Use the internet for studying and observing performance mediums.
- Learn to recognise instruments/voices.
- Learn to identify chords and cadences by playing them on piano/guitar.
- Complete past exam papers and workbook exercises.
- Be familiar with a range of major and minor key signatures.

If a question asks you to identify the texture of a piece of music, try to give some detail about the melody **and** the accompaniment, if present.

Musical Features and Techniques

Melodic features refer to the treatment of the tune. For example:

- Step movement
- Chromatic movement
- Sequences
- Blues/jazz notes (flattened third or seventh notes of a major scale)
- Wide leaps
- Repeated notes
- Arpeggio/triadic movement
- Repetition

Rhythmic features refer only to the rhythm. For example:

- Changing time signatures
- Syncopation
- Steady rhythm
- Dotted rhythm
- Ostinato (repeated rhythmic pattern)

Harmonic features refer to what is happening in the accompaniment/harmony. For example:

- Major/minor/diminished chords
- Sustained/block/broken/Alberti chords
- Homophonic/polyphonic textures
- Dissonant sounds

Compositional techniques refer to the musical devices used by the composer. They may include all of the features mentioned above, as well as:

- Modulation
- Pedal note
- Canon
- Imitation
- Antiphony
- Inversion
- Augmentation
- Contrary motion

Instrumental techniques refer to the way by which an instrument is played. For example:

- Pizzicato
- Arco
- Con/senza sordino
- Col legno
- Vibrato
- Glissando

The Exam

On the day of the exam:

1. **Attempt to answer all the questions, even if you don't know the answer.** Try not to leave any blanks, as you could pick up a mark or two if you write something.
2. **Read the questions very carefully.** Underline key words in a question. For example: *Name the instruments that play the* _melody_ *in this excerpt.*
3. **Tick the correct number of boxes.** If a question asks for one feature, only tick one box. You could be penalised if you tick too many or too few boxes.
4. **Make notes on musical features in the excerpts.** Students are often asked to compare one musical excerpt with another. If you have time, make notes on what you hear in the music as it is being played. You may have to refer to this music later in the question.
5. Be clear with **underline or circle instructions.** If your answer is unclear, you may lose marks.
6. When asked to **identify a cadence point**, answer with the appropriate term such as perfect, imperfect, etc. The exam usually specifies not to use Roman numerals in your answer.
7. **Stay relaxed and focused.** Remember, you will hear everything three times, so you don't need to rush.

Leaving Certificate Examination 2020, Question 6

This question is based on four excerpts of music. Answer the questions on each excerpt. Use the tips provided to help you.

Go to www.examinations.ie/exammaterialarchive to access the musical excerpts featured in this question.

Select the following file: Exam Papers > 2020 > Leaving Certificate > Music > Paper Two: Sound File

Excerpt	Question	Answer guide
Excerpt 1, played twice. An outline score of bars 1–8 of this excerpt is printed below.	*(music score, bars 1–8, with X marked between bars 6 and 7)*	
	(a) Insert the four missing notes at **X** on the score.	• This is a **dictation** question. • Follow the score that is given. • You might like to make a note of the direction of the missing notes or jot the rhythm over the top of the missing bar. • Is the missing bar a repeat of a previous bar?
Excerpt 1, played twice more.	(b) Name the instruments that play the melody in this excerpt.	• Underline the **key word**: melody. • Can you identify the family of instruments? • What about timbre (high, medium or low pitch)?
	(c) The form of the music heard in this excerpt is ☐ ABA ☐ ABB ☐ ABC	• The music fits into three 8-bar structures. • Can you hear a repeat of any of the phrases? • Is there a different phrase at the end? If not, you can eliminate ABC.
Excerpt 2, played three times.	(d) Describe the texture of the music in this excerpt. _____ _____ _____	• There are three blank lines given for this answer, so you will need more than a one-word answer for full marks. • Is the music **polyphonic**, **homophonic** or **monophonic**? • Describe what instruments are playing and what they are playing (melody, countermelody, accompaniment).

Excerpt	Question	Answer guide
Excerpt 3, played three times.	Line 1 Joyful, joyful, Lord we adore Thee. Line 2 God of glory, God of love. Line 3 Hearts unfold like flowers before Thee, Line 4 Hail Thee as the sun above. Line 5 Melt the clouds of sin and sadness, Line 6 Drive the dark of doubt away. Line 7 Giver of immortal gladness, Line 8 Fill us with the light, fill us with the light. Line 9 Oh, fill us with the light of day.	
	(e) The rhythm of the introduction played on piano is ☐ ♩ ♩ ♩ ♩ | ♩ ♩ ♩ ☐ ♩ ♩ ♩ ♩ | ♩. ♪ ♩ ☐ ♩ ♩ ♩ ♩ | ♩ ♩	• Only tick one box here. • Check this answer each time the excerpt is played.
	(f) Describe one similarity between the vocal music of line 1 and the vocal music of line 3. _____ _____ _____ _____	• Underline the word **similarity**. • Make very small one-word notes on the page. • Consider tempo, style of singing and cadence.
	(g) Identify the cadence at the end of line 6. _____ _____	• Answer using one of the terms: **perfect**, **imperfect**, **plagal** or **interrupted**. • Do not use Roman numerals.

Excerpt	Question	Answer guide
	(h) There is a climax in the music in line 7. How is this achieved?	• Underline the word **climax**. • A musical climax can be achieved in many ways, including change of tempo, change of dynamics, change of pitch or change of instrumentation. Can you hear any of these features in the excerpt?
Excerpt 4, played three times.	(i) Describe two differences between the music heard in this excerpt and the music heard in Excerpt 3. Refer to both excerpts in your answer. 1. _____ 2. _____	• Answer this question in very clear and concise language. • Consider any instruments that have been added or taken away, tempo changes, texture changes, key changes, etc. • Refer to both excerpts in your answer. For example: Excerpt 3 features a solo singer, whereas Excerpt 4 has a choir. **See page 171 for the marking scheme to this question.**

Aural Skills Key Words

Performance Details

Dynamics	How music is played, e.g. loud, soft, and transitions between.
Phrasing/articulation	How notes are played, e.g. legato (smooth), staccato (choppy), flowing or disjointed.
Tempo	The speed at which the music is played, e.g. fast, slow, moderate.

Texture

Dense texture	Many instruments playing.
Homophonic	One line of melody with harmonic accompaniment.
Light texture	Few instruments playing, light harmonic accompaniment.
Monophonic	A single line of melody, no harmonic accompaniment.
Polyphonic/ Contrapuntal	Two or more independent melodic lines. Examples: ● Descant (melody heard over main melody) ● Countermelody (a second melody played in counterpoint with the main melody) ● Canon (one or more voices strictly imitate each other at a fixed distance) ● Fugue (a melody is introduced then all parts imitate the main melody in turn).

Form

Binary	Two-part form: AB, AABB, ABAB.
Free form	Unrecognisable form structure.
Ritornello	A musical form where the main theme returns between different episodes.
Rondo	The main theme returns after each contrasting phrase: ABACA.
Sonata form	Large-scale ternary form: exposition, development, recapitulation, coda.
Strophic	The music is the same for each verse.
Ternary	Three phrases or sections: ABA, AABA, ABBA.
Theme and variations	A theme can be varied in different ways, e.g. changing melody, harmony, tonality, rhythm, etc.
Through composed	The music is different for each verse.

Common Musical Terms

Antiphony	Where two groups of voices/instruments imitate each other in quick succession; 'call and answer'.
Block chord	Chord notes played together at the same time.

Broken chord	Notes of a chord played in succession.
Imitation	Melody imitated by another instrument/voice.
Ostinato	A melodic/rhythmic phrase that is repeated identically several times.
Pedal note	A note held or repeated over several bars while the harmony changes.
Repetition	Melody/rhythm repeated by the same instrument.
Sequence	Melody repeated (by the same instrument) at a higher or lower pitch.
Syncopation	Placing emphasis on the offbeat.
Timbre	The tone quality of sound, a musical note or tone.

The Orchestra

Chamber	15 to 45 players, often used for Baroque and Classical music.
Pop	Orchestral instruments with added guitar, drumkit and keyboards.
String	String players only.
Symphony	Up to 100 players.

By Period

Baroque (1600–1750)	Small string section: violins, viola, cello, double bass, flute, oboe, trumpet, harpsichord or organ.
Classical (1750–1800)	Larger string section than Baroque era, with flute, oboe, bassoon, clarinet, horn, trumpets, timpani.
Romantic (1800–1900)	Large string section with harp, piccolo, flutes, oboes, cor anglais, clarinets, bass clarinet, bassoons, double bassoon, up to four horns, up to three trumpets, trombones, tuba.
Modern (1900–present)	Same as romantic orchestra with percussion instruments such as snare drum, xylophone, piano, tambourine.

Vocal Music

A cappella	Unaccompanied singing.
Falsetto	Male voice singing in an artificially high register.
Glissando	Sliding from one note to another.

Melismatic word setting	Several notes sung per syllable.
Syllabic word setting	One note sung per syllable.
Vibrato	Fluctuation in pitch creating a quivering sound.

Voices

Soprano	Highest female voice.
Mezzo soprano	Female voice with a range between soprano and alto.
Alto/contralto	Lowest female voice.
Tenor	Highest male voice.
Baritone	Male voice with a range between tenor and bass.
Bass	Lowest male voice.

Instrumental Techniques

Arco	Use the bow (instruction after *pizz.*).
Col legno	Use the wood of the bow.
Con sordino	With mute.
Fanfare	Declamatory flourish, played by brass, usually at ceremonial occasions.
Glissando	Slide from one note to the next.
Harmonics	A note produced on a string instrument by touching the string lightly at a particular point.
Pizzicato	Plucking the string.
Senza sordino	Without mute.
Sul ponticello	Play near the bridge (string instrument).
Sul tastiera	Play near/on the fingerboard.
Tremolando	Rapid, repeated bowing on the same note.
Vibrato	Quivering effect achieved by moving the fingers on the left hand, resulting in slight pitch fluctuations.

Marking Scheme Question 6 (2020) Higher Level

Excerpt 1: Finale, Ode, 'To Joy' from Symphony No. 9 in D minor by Beethoven

(a)

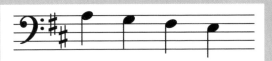

    0.5 × 4 for pitch and rhythm. Both pitch & rhythm must be correct.
Mark the first 4 notes from left to right in bar 6   (2 marks)

(b) Cello and double bass
Allow viola   (1+1 marks)

(c) ABB   (2 marks)

Excerpt 2: Finale, Ode, 'To Joy' from Symphony No. 9 in D minor by Beethoven

(d) Up to 3 marks for a valid description of the texture of the music in this excerpt. For example: polyphonic + elaboration; two (three) different melodies can be heard at the same time (violins + bassoon + bass); countermelody on bassoon against lower strings; countermelody on bassoon against violins

N.B. Reference to polyphonic/countermelody not necessary for full marks   (3 marks)

Excerpt 3: 'Joyful Joyful' from Sister Act

(e)   (2 marks)

(f) Up to 2 marks for a description of one valid similarity between the vocal music of line 1 and line 3

Partially correct answer = 1 mark   (2 marks)

(g) Imperfect
Allow perfect   (1 mark)

(h) Up to 2 marks for a description of how a climax is achieved in the music in line 7

Partially correct answer = 1 mark   (2 marks)

Excerpt 4: 'Joyful Joyful' from Sister Act

(i) Up to 2 marks for each for description of two valid differences between the music heard in Excerpt 4 and the music heard in Excerpt 3. Answers must refer to both excerpts.

Reference to difference in lyrics = 0
Partially correct answer = 1 mark   (2+2 marks)

(20 marks)

4 Music Theory and Terminology

aims

By the end of this chapter, you will be able to:

- understand the requirements for the composition paper
- understand the different choices of melody and harmony that are available on the paper
- understand what is needed to attain high marks in the melody and harmony questions
- identify different ways in which the melody and harmony questions may appear on the paper

The composition paper is worth 100 marks.

Students are required to complete one melody question (40 marks) and one harmony question (60 marks).

The time allocated for the composition paper is 1 hour and 30 minutes.

Students must be familiar with the following key signatures.

Major Key			Minor Key		
C major	0		A minor	0	
G major	1 #	F#	E minor	1 #	F#
D major	2 #	F#, C#	B minor	2 #	F#, C#
A major	3 #	F#, C#, G#	F# minor	3 #	F#, C#, G#
E major	4 #	F#, C#, G#, D#	C# minor	4 #	F#, C#, G#, D#
F major	1♭	B♭	D minor	1♭	B♭
B♭ major	2♭	B♭, E♭	G minor	2♭	B♭, E♭
E♭ major	3♭	B♭, E♭, A♭	C minor	3♭	B♭, E♭, A♭
A♭ major	4♭	B♭, E♭, A♭, D♭	F minor	4♭	B♭, E♭, A♭, D♭

C major / A minor	G major / E minor	D major / B minor	A major / F# minor	E major / C# minor
No sharps or flats	F#	F#, C#	F#, C#, G#	F#, C#, G#, D#

F major / D minor	B♭ major / G minor	E♭ major / C minor	A♭ major / F minor
B♭	B♭, E♭	B♭, E♭, A♭	B♭, E♭, A♭, D♭

Students are commonly asked to write a melody in any one of the following time signatures:

The symbol **C** or **common time** is the same as 4/4 time.

The symbol **¢** or **cut common time** is the same as 2/2 time.

Basic Music Theory

This chapter will focus on the basic music theory and terminology necessary for the Leaving Certificate Music syllabus.

As a Leaving Certificate Music student, you may have already taken classes in singing or in an instrument outside of school for many years. Alternatively, you may have decided to take Music as a subject in Fifth Year without any previous musical experience or background knowledge. Either way, it is important to get a good grounding in the basics of musical theory.

If you are new to reading music, or you want to brush up on your skills, the internet is an invaluable resource. From beginners' videos on YouTube to more advanced written musical theory, it is easy to find lessons suitable for your level. Try searching for 'music theory beginner', 'music theory exercise' or 'music theory revision'.

Pitch

There are several **clefs** in music that are used to establish pitch. The **treble clef** and the **bass clef** are the most common.

Treble clef or G clef   Bass clef or F clef

The clefs are placed on the set of five lines and four spaces known as the **stave**.

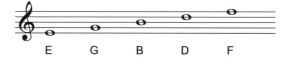

E   G   B   D   F

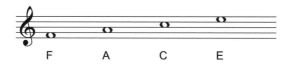

F   A   C   E

The **treble clef** is used for voices or instruments that sound medium- to high-pitch notes.

The **bass clef** is used for voices or instruments that sound low-pitch notes.

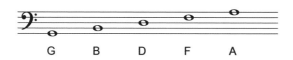

G   B   D   F   A

A   C   E   G

Tones and Semitones

The distance between each note can be measured in steps called **tones** and **semitones**. **A semitone is the smallest distance between two notes.** There are two semitones in a tone. It is easier to understand this by looking at the notes on a piano keyboard. Let's focus on the scale of C major, which consists of all the white keys on the piano.

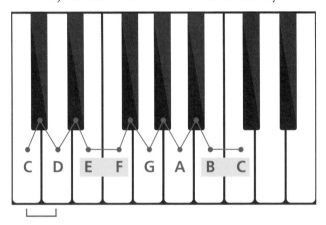

The notes with a black key between them are **tones**. The notes without a black key between them are **semitones**.

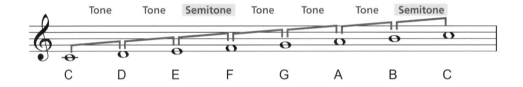

#, ♭ and ♮ Symbols

(sharp), ♭ (flat) and ♮ (natural) are symbols that raise or lower the pitch of the note. They can appear next to the clef as a **key signature**, in which case they apply to the entire piece of music, or next to individual notes, where they are called **accidentals**.

Think of the white notes on the piano as **natural** (♮) notes. Look at the note G on the piano keyboard.

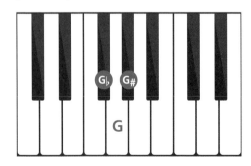

By moving 'up' in pitch by a semitone, G becomes G#.

By moving 'down' in pitch by a semitone, G becomes G♭.

Note Values

The most used notes values in music are shown in the table below.

Note			Rest		
	Semibreve	4 beats		Bar rest	Whole bar
	Minim	2 beats			2 beats
	Crotchet	1 beat		Crotchet rest	1 beat
	Quaver	½ beat		Quaver rest	½ beat
	Semiquaver	¼ beat		Semiquaver rest	¼ beat

Dotted Notes

The dot adds half of the value onto the note that is in front of the dot.

3 beats   =

1 + ½ beat   =

¾ beat   =

Time Signatures

Time signatures are used to tell us how many **beats** to count in each bar. A time signature is found at the start of the stave and after a key signature (see below). A time signature has two numbers, one on top of the other.

The top number tells us how many beats are in each bar.

The bottom number tells us what type of beat to count in. A '4' on the bottom represents crotchet beats, a '2' represents minim beats, and so on.

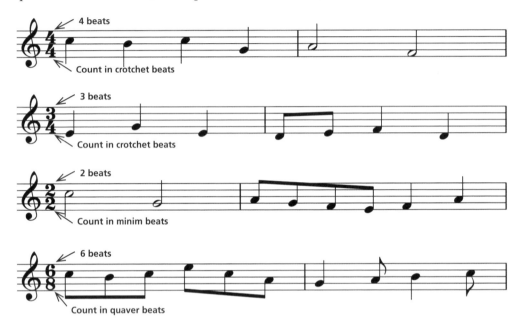

Simple Time Signatures

Time signatures can be either **simple** or **compound**.

Simple time signatures are the easiest to count and play. The pulse or the steady beat can be counted in groups of 1 or 2.

$\frac{2}{2}$	2 minim beats per bar	$\frac{2}{4}$	2 crotchet beats per bar	$\frac{2}{8}$	2 quaver beats per bar
$\frac{3}{2}$	3 minim beats per bar	$\frac{3}{4}$	3 crotchet beats per bar	$\frac{3}{8}$	3 quaver beats per bar
$\frac{4}{2}$	4 minim beats per bar	$\frac{4}{4}$	4 crotchet beats per bar	$\frac{4}{8}$	4 quaver beats per bar

Compound Time Signatures

The pulse in compound time is the value of a **dotted note**. The most common compound time signatures are shown in the table below.

6/4	2 dotted minim beats per bar	**6/8**	2 dotted crotchet beats per bar	**6/16**	2 dotted quaver beats per bar
9/4	3 dotted minim beats per bar	**9/8**	3 dotted crotchet beats per bar	**9/16**	3 dotted quaver beats per bar
12/4	4 dotted minim beats per bar	**12/8**	4 dotted crotchet beats per bar	**12/16**	4 dotted quaver beats per bar

Key Signatures

Key signatures are the # or ♭ symbols that are found after the clef on a piece of music. A key signature represents the **tonal centre** of the music. A tonal centre can be **major** or **minor**.

Major and minor keys share key signatures, as shown below.

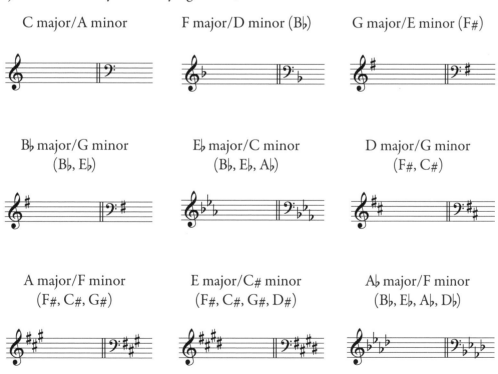

C major/A minor

F major/D minor (B♭)

G major/E minor (F#)

B♭ major/G minor (B♭, E♭)

E♭ major/C minor (B♭, E♭, A♭)

D major/G minor (F#, C#)

A major/F minor (F#, C#, G#)

E major/C# minor (F#, C#, G#, D#)

A♭ major/F minor (B♭, E♭, A♭, D♭)

For the composition paper you should be able to compose a melody and harmony in any key up to and including four #s and four ♭s.

Tempo

The tempo is the **speed** of the music. Here are some common terms used to describe tempo.

A tempo	Return to original speed.
Accelerando	Becoming faster.
Adagio	Very slow.
Andante	At a walking pace.
Andantino	Slightly faster than andante.
Allegro	Lively.
Animé	At a moderately quick tempo.
Grave	Very slow.
Lento	Slow.
Moderato	At a moderate pace.
Meno mosso	Less movement.
Piú mosso	More movement.
Presto	Quick.
Rallentando	Becoming slower.
Ritardando	Gradually becoming slower.
Vivace	Lively and brisk.

Dynamics

Dynamics indicate the **volume** of the music. Common terms and symbols used to describe dynamics are explained below.

Piano	p	Soft
Mezzo piano	mp	Moderately soft
Pianissimo	pp	Very soft
Forte	f	Loud
Mezzo forte	mf	Moderately loud
Fortissimo	ff	Very loud
Crescendo	cresc.	Gradually getting louder
Decrescendo/ diminuendo	dim.	Gradually getting softer

Articulation

Articulation refers to how notes should be **played**. Are they long and broad, or short and choppy? A composer uses different signs and terms to instruct the singer or player on how to sound the notes. Here are some examples of common forms of articulation.

Word	Symbol	Definition
Staccato		Short, choppy note
Legato		Play notes smoothly
Accent		Stress the note
Marcato		Play note with force

Tenuto		Play the note for its full value
Fermata		Pause, hold the note

Intervals

An **interval** is the distance between two notes, from the lowest to the highest. It is measured in the number of semitones between the two notes. Here is an example:

Interval Name	Distance between Notes	Example
Major 2nd	1 tone	C–D
Major 3rd	2 tones	C–E
Perfect 4th	2 tones and 1 semitone	C–F
Perfect 5th	3 tones and 1 semitone	C–G
Major 6th	4 tones and 1 semitone	C–A
Major 7th	5 tones and 1 semitone	C–B
Perfect octave	6 tones	C–C'

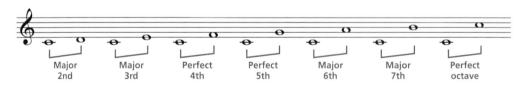

A **minor** interval is a semitone **lower** than a major interval.

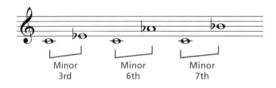

A **diminished** interval is a semitone **lower** than a perfect interval.

Diminished
5th

An **augmented** interval is a semitone **higher** than a major or a perfect interval.

Augmented
4th

For more on musical theory, revise Chapter 3: Aural Skills.

5 Melody

aims By the end of this chapter, you will be able to:
- understand the best approaches to melody writing
- understand and recognise different ways the melody question may be presented
- understand what is required to achieve high marks in the melody question

There are several possible approaches to the melody composition section of the Leaving Certificate examination paper. Students must complete one out of the three choices of melody question on the composition paper.

When working on melody writing, it is advisable that you take primary direction from your teacher.

Question 1: Continue the given opening to make a suitable 16-bar melody.

or

Question 2: An opening line has been set to music. Set the remaining words to make a melody of 16 bars.

or

Question 3: Continue the given dance rhythm to make a 16-bar melody.

Question 1

Most Leaving Certificate students opt for Question 1 in the melody section of the composition paper. This requires the student to develop a given opening into a 16-bar melody.

REQUIREMENTS FOR QUESTION 1:
- Add 12 bars to an existing four-bar phrase
- Modulate to the dominant at a suitable point (in the **major** key only)
- Add suitable phrasing and dynamics
- Choose a suitable instrument of your choice (a choice of four instruments given on the paper)

There are various methods of structuring a composition for Question 1. The two most popular are:

- Adding 12 bars using **tonic solfa** (tonic solfa is a method of singing the notes of a scale: do, re, mi, etc.).
- Adding 12 bars by following a harmonic template.

Whatever method you use to compose a melody, you must remember the key features required for a musical outcome. Your added 12 bars **must** musically connect to the four given bars.

A H1 grade in the melody question requires 34–40 marks. To achieve these marks, your work must meet the following requirements:

- Melody and rhythm have excellent style and imagination
- Excellent shape and structure
- Excellent development of opening ideas
- Excellent sense of direction and climax
- Appropriate performing directions (phrasing and dynamics) inserted
- Suitable instrument chosen

What you need to do to achieve a H1 in melody writing:

- It is important that you have a **strong sense of what the opening phrase sounds like.**
- Your melody must **sound musically connected** to the given phrase.
- There needs to be a **natural flow** in the rhythm and the melody.
- Your melody should have an audible **beginning, middle and end.**

When trying to establish an excellent sense of direction and climax, plot your melody as you would write a story or a movie script:

- Bars 1–4: Introduce the main characters and establish a plot.
- Bars 5–8: Develop the characters and the plot (develop opening idea and modulation).
- Bars 9–12: Begin the exciting part of the story (B phrase, something slightly different to the opening building up to the most dramatic part of the melody).
- Bars 13–16: Bring the story to a satisfying finale (return to the A phrase with a final ending).

The four given bars in Question 1 may be in any of the major or minor keys up to and including 4 #s and 4 ♭s. They may be in 4/4, 2/4, 3/4, 2/2 or 6/8 time.

There may also be an **anacrusis** (upbeat).

Instrument Choice

You are given a choice of four instruments on the paper. These will likely be a selection of the following:

- Violin
- Flute
- Oboe
- Clarinet
- Descant recorder
- Horn
- Trumpet

Range of Instruments

Consider the range of each instrument presented before you start composing to ensure that they have the range required for your idea.

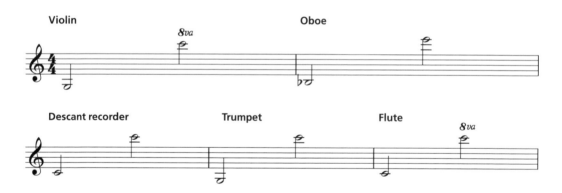

Be careful not to write beyond the range of your chosen instrument, as this will affect your marks.

Keep in mind the register of the given phrase; if you write in a very high register, this may not musically connect to the given material.

Note that there may be any number of bars on the first system (line) given.

Before you start to compose your melody:

1. Number each bar and mark in phrasing (see example below).
2. Decide on what **form** or structure you will use. Question 1 melodies commonly use A–A1–B–A2 or A–A1–B–B1 structure.
3. Add **phrase marks** when mapping out bars.
4. Identify the key signature correctly.
5. Establish the **correct modulation** to the dominant key.
6. Pencil in your **modulation point** to the dominant key.
7. Plan strong cadence points (at the end of each phrase).

Structure at a Glance

	A–A1–B–A2	A–A1–B–B1
Bars 1–4 (given material)	A	A
Bars 5–8	A1	A1
Bars 9–12	B	B
Bars 13–16	A2	B1

exam TIPS

An accidental in the given music may suggest that the melody is in the minor key.

If the question states that you must modulate to the dominant at a suitable point, then the melody is in the major key. You are **not** required to modulate in the minor key.

Major Melody

Using Tonic Solfa to Compose a Melody

1. Write out the scale of the tonic key.
2. Identify the dominant (fifth note, or 'soh' of the tonic scale).
3. Raise the fifth note one semitone to change the modulation from 'fah' to 'fe'.

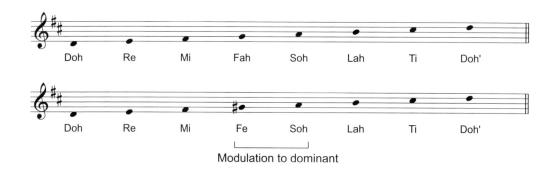

Sample Template for Using Chordal Pattern in the Major Key

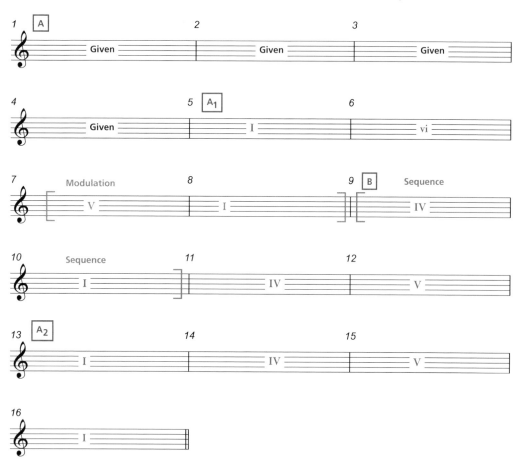

Leaving Certificate Examination 2019, Question 1

Question 1 from the 2019 Higher Level Music Leaving Certificate Exam is a melody question in the key of A♭ major. There are a number of features in this question that you can study in preparation for a potential major melody question: it has an upbeat, a challenging opening rhythm pattern and a modulation to a key with flats. Below is a step-by-step guide to answering this question successfully.

exam Q

SECTION A – MELODY COMPOSITION (40 MARKS)

Question	Answer guide
Q.1 Continuation of a given opening	• Continue the opening below to make a 16-bar melody. • Include a modulation to the dominant at a suitable point. • Add appropriate performing directions (phrasing and dynamics) to the melody. • Choose a suitable instrument for your melody from the following list: ☐ horn ☐ violin ☐ clarinet ☐ flute

Moderato

mf

Before You Start

1. Establish the tonic and dominant key.

   Tonic = A♭ major

   Dominant (modulating key) = E♭ major

2. Write out scales with modulation and/or chord boxes in both keys.

Doh   Re   Mi   Fah   Soh   Lah   Ti   Doh'

Soh   Lah   Ti   Doh   Re   Mi   Fe   Soh

Tonic						
Ab major has four ♭s: Bb, Eb, Ab, Db						

Notes of Chord						
Eb	F	G	Ab	Db	C	Db
C	Db	Eb	F	Bb	Ab	Bb
Ab	Bb	C	Db	G	F	G
				Eb		

Chord Symbol						
Ab	Bbm	Cm	Db	Eb	Fm	G°

Roman Numeral						
I	ii	iii	IV	V	vi	vii°

Dominant						
Eb major has three ♭s: Bb, Eb, Ab (Db is raised to D)						

Notes of Chord						
Bb	C	D	Ab	Ab	G	Ab
G	Ab	Bb	F	F	Eb	F
Eb	F	G	Db	D♮	C	Db
				Bb		

Chord Symbol						
Eb	Fm	Gm	Ab	Bb	Cm	Db

Roman Numeral						
I	ii	iii	IV	V(7)	vi	vii°

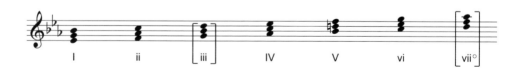

Developing the Given Material and the A Phrases

- It is very important that your 12 bars make a musical connection with the given phrase.
- Practise drafting variations of bars 1 and 2, bars 3 and 4. Try to keep a sense of the rhythm from bars one and two in bars 13 and 14.
- Mark in the tonic solfa of the given bars and/or the harmonic structure.
- Analyse melodic features used in the given phrase. For example: Does it have a lot of step movement? Are there leaps in the melody? Are there any repeated notes?
- Be aware of any anacrusis/upbeat.

Analysis of given phrase

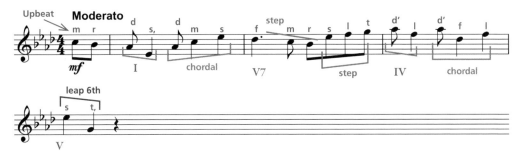

Step 1: Bars 1 and 2

- Analyse the given opening bars by marking in tonic solfa and/or chords used. This will give you a good sense of how the melody sounds, which is crucial in achieving a high grade.
- Identify and highlight the melodic features. Here, we have an upbeat, some chordal movements and some step movement. You may use these features to develop your melody.

Step 2: Rhythm of bars 1 and 2

Mark out the rhythm of the opening bars.

This should also be factored into the development of the opening bars.

Variation 1:

Variation 1 is developed from the chords I (bar 1) and VI (bar 2). The rhythm of bar 1 is changed in bar 5 by adding a **passing note** between C and E♭. The rhythm of bar 6 is the same as that of bar 2, though the melody itself is structured around the VI chord (F minor).

Variation 2:

In variation 2, the rhythm from bars 1 and 2 has been adapted to create a musical connection in bars 5 and 6. Note that the melody in bar 6 has been adapted from that of bar 2.

Step 3: Modulation to the dominant

- Bars 7 and 8 in the A1 phrase is a good point to plot a modulation.
- It is important that you have a strong cadential point at the end of bar 8. This can be done successfully by having a V–I cadence in the new key.
- Make sure to end your phrase on the new key note.
- Check the bars for the correct accidental.

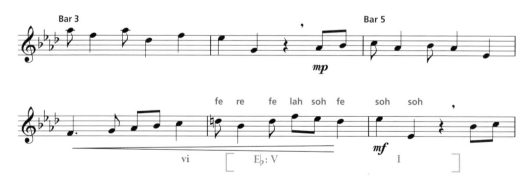

Step 4: The B phrase, bars 9–12

- A common compositional technique used in the B phrase is a **sequence**. A sequence is repetition of a musical pattern at a higher or lower pitch. This can be written by using tonic solfa and/or a specific chordal sequence. The sample below shows how you might incorporate this idea into your melody.
- Bar 9 starts on the tonic solfa note *fah*; bar 10 repeats bar 9 but one note lower, starting on *mi*.
- Bar 11 leads up to a dramatic cadential point in bar 12.
- Remember to incorporate a sense of structure and phrasing.

After studying the rhythm and melody of the given phrase, mark out the next 12 bars and label your phrase (e.g. A–A1–B–A2). Add a phrase mark directly after the last note/rest in the given phrase.

Make sure to count four bars in each phrase and **watch out for the upbeat if there is one**; your new phrase will start after each upbeat.

Try to write outside of the range of the given phrase. Note that in the example above there is a higher register used from bar 11. This, along with the crescendo, adds to the sense of climax in the music.

Other ideas for writing a B phrase

These ideas are **not a requirement of the question** but can produce effective and melodic B phrases.

- Modulating to the relative minor in bars 9 and 10. For example:

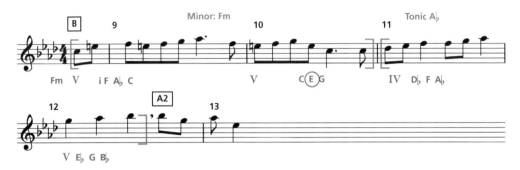

Relative minor = F minor

Notes of Chord	C A♭ F	D♭ B♭ G	E♮ C A♭	F D♭ B♭	B♭ G E♮ C	A♭ F D♭	B♭ G E
Chord Symbol	Fm	Go	A♭+	B♭m	C	D♭	E°
Roman Numeral	i	ii°	III+	iv	V(7)	VI	vii°

- Modulate to subdominant, then dominant. This can be tricky and would require some practice. For example:

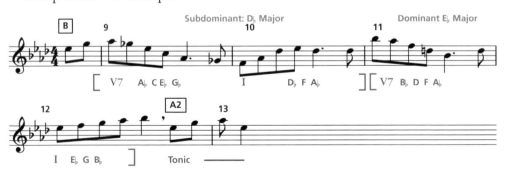

Subdominant = D♭ major						
				G♭		
A♭	B♭	C	D♭	E♭	F	G♭
F	G	A♭	B♭	C	D♭	E♭
D♭	E♭	F	G♭	A♭	B♭	C
D♭	E♭m	Fm	G♭	A♭7	B♭m	C°
I	ii	iii	IV	V(7)	vi	vii°

Dominant = E♭ major						
				A♭		
B♭	C	D	E♭	F	G	A♭
G	A♭	B♭	C	D	E♭	F
E♭	F	G	A♭	B♭	C	D
E♭	Fm	Gm	A♭	B♭7	C	D
I	ii	iii	IV	V	vi	vii

exam focus

Leaving Certificate Examination 2019, Question 1: Sample Answer

Points to note:

- Note the treatment of the upbeat: each new phrase starts with an upbeat and musically connects to the next bar.
- The last bar and upbeat should make up one full bar.
- Check that you have the correct amount of beats in every bar.
- Check that your composition makes a musical connection with the given phrase.
- Include strong cadential points at the end of every phrase.
- Include a modulation to the dominant at a suitable point.
- Add in musical use of dynamics and phrasing.
- End on tonic note.

> Bars 1 and 3 in the given phrase use the same rhythmic pattern. It is **syncopated**, so the emphasis is on the off beat. You could incorporate the syncopated notes into your developing bars to keep a strong musical connection with the given phrase.

Minor Melody

You are **not** required to modulate in the minor key.

- It is important that you understand how to write in the minor key.
- It is important to have strong cadences at the end of each phrase.
- Practice writing out and learning all minor scales up to and including four #s and four ♭s.
- Be careful how you use the raised seventh in the minor key. Try to avoid the interval of an augmented second.

D minor scale

The melodic minor scale: the raised sixth and raised seventh approaching the tonic does not contain an augmented interval and makes for a strong V–I cadence point.

Raised 6th and raised 7th approaching the tonic D

Below is a suggested chord template that you may adapt to your minor key melody.

End of tonic

Leaving Certificate Examination 2016, Question 1: Sample Answer

Leaving Certificate Examination 2020, Question 1: Sample Answer

When composing in 6/8 time, it is important to keep a pulse of two strong beats in the bar.

A 6/8 rhythm consists of two groups of three quavers. Be mindful of this when composing the rhythm.

Suggested rhythmic patterns in 6/8:

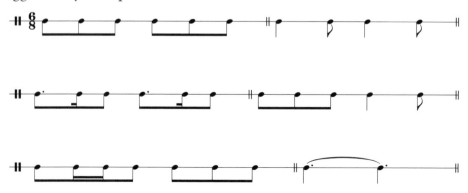

Points to note:

- In order to achieve optimum marks in the melody question, your composition must have excellent shape and structure. It must have some dynamics and a strong musical connection to the given phrase.
- Mark phrasing with either ' at the end of each phrase or a line.
- You may add articulation and bowing (if violin is your chosen instrument) but it is not required. It is important that you continue in the style of the given bars.
- Make sure you have dynamics that make musical sense, and don't overdo it – it's only 16 bars.
- Include a climactic point in your composition. This may be done by writing above the range of the given phrase.
- Double-check that you have the correct number of beats in the bar, and that you have modulated correctly.

Question 2

Setting Music to a Given Text

In this question, students are usually given four lines of a poem to set to music.

The opening line of the music is given.

The text will determine the rhythm and flow of the melody, and the mood of the text should be reflected in the music.

Question 3

Composing to a Given Dance Rhythm or Metre or Form

This question is similar to Question 1, except you are required to write in the form and style of a particular dance.

The form is usually A–A1–B–B1.

It is important to know rhythmic features and styles of dances such as gigue, minuet, trio, gavotte and waltz.

6 Harmony

The harmony question is worth 60 marks.

Students must complete one out of the three choices of harmony questions on the composition paper.

exam Q

Question 4: Compose a melody and bass notes from a set of chords.

or

Question 5: Compose bass notes and chord indications to a given tune.

or

Question 6: Add a countermelody or descant and chordal support to a given tune.

WHICH QUESTION SHOULD I CHOOSE?

- Question 5 is a popular choice, as students can gain a lot of marks from choosing appropriate chords and good-quality chord progressions.
- Questions 4 and 6 require you to compose a melody or countermelody, so these questions are best suited to students with strong melody-writing skills.

You must demonstrate a knowledge of chords and chord progressions in all three of the harmony questions. You may use Roman numerals or chord symbols when writing your chords.

Chords

Root Position Chords

Each harmony question requires you to understand the construction of major and minor key chords, up to and including four sharps (#) and four flats (♭).

You may represent your harmony choices by using Roman numerals or chord symbols.

Major Key Chords

- In a major key, the chords of I, IV and V are **major chords**.
- The chords of ii, iii and iv are **minor chords**.
- The chord of VII° is a **diminished chord** and should be avoided.

A♭ major has four ♭s: B♭, E♭, A♭, D♭

Notes of Chord					D♭		
	E♭	F	G	A♭	B♭	C	D♭
	C	D♭	E♭	F	G	A♭	B♭
	A♭	B♭	C	D♭	E♭	F	G
Chord Symbol	A♭	B♭m	Cm	D♭	E♭	Fm	Go
Roman Numeral	I	ii	iii	IV	V(7)	vi	VII°

Minor Key Chords

- In a minor key, the chords of i and iv are **minor chords**.
- The chords of V and VI are **major chords**.
- The chord of II° is a **diminished chord**. This chord is only to be used in 1st inversion.
- The chord of III+ is an **augmented chord** and should be avoided.

C minor has two ♭s: E♭, A♭ (B♭ is raised to B♮)

Notes of Chord					F		
	G	A♭	B♮	C	D	E♭	F
	E♭	F	G	A♭	B♮	C	D
	C	D	E♭	F	G	A♭	B♮
Chord Symbol	Cm	Do	E♭+	Fm	G	A♭	B°
Roman Numeral	i	ii°	III+	iv	V(7)	VI	vii°

The Basics of Harmony

- Choose to use either chord symbol or Roman numeral.
- Be familiar with notating the bass in the bass clef.
- Do not use the same chord, in the same position in two adjacent boxes.
- Use appropriate chord symbols; insert 'm' for minor and the relevant ♭ or # signs.
- When using Roman numerals, use upper case for major chords and lower case for minor chords.
- Bass notes of each chord symbol must match the chord symbol/Roman numeral.

		Major Key	Minor Key
Finished	**Perfect**	V V7–I	V V7–i
	Plagal	IV–I	iv–i
Unfinished	**Imperfect**	Any chord to V or V7	Any chord to V or V7
	Interrupted	V–vi	V–VI

A cadence point marks the end of a phrase. The last two chords of a piece will make a finished cadence.

It is likely that the harmony question will have phrases that are four bars long, but do not rely on this.

Try to sing and/or tap out the rhythm of the given melody in order to identify a cadence point.

Chord Progressions

A chord progression is the movement from one chord to another. In Question 5, over half of the marks are dependent on the use of strong chord progressions that fit with the given melody.

Below are a number of strong and common chord progressions.

1. **All cadence progressions**
2. **Chords that fall a third in the bass. A good example of this is the chord progression I–vi–IV–ii.**

3. **Chords that rise a fourth in the bass, for example; I–IV, ii–V.**

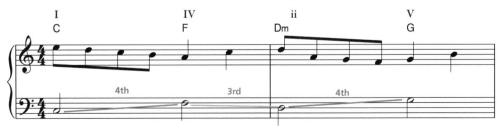

4. The chord of I can move to any chord: ii, IV, V or vi.

5. The chord of IV can move to I, ii, or V.

6. The chord of V can move to I, IV, V7 or vi.

PROGRESSIONS TO AVOID WHERE POSSIBLE:

• ii–I

• V–ii

• V7–V

The Dominant Seventh

The chord V7, or the **dominant 7th**, is the chord of V with the seventh note added. This can be treated as a separate chord to the chord of V. It can sound very strong when it follows V in the same bar.

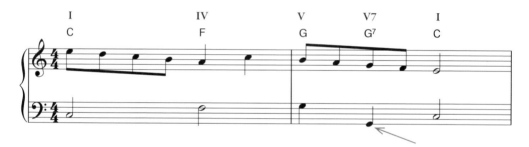

When using the chord V7, note that the root of the chord is in the bass.

First Inversion Chords

First inversion chords occur when the third note of the chord is heard in the bass. First inversions provide an added choice to the harmony. Although they are musically effective, they are not as strong as root position chords and should be used with care.

There are a number of points to remember when using first inversion chords:

• First inversion chords usually occur between two root position chords.

• All chords can be used in first inversion.

• In the minor key, the chord of ii° may only be used in first inversion, ii°b.

• The chord of **Vb is commonly followed by the chord I**, unless the bass line descends from the tonic note : I–Vb–vi.

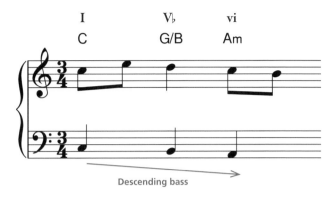

Descending bass

- Avoid doubling the third note of the chord when composing in the major key. If the third of the chord is in the treble, avoid using the first inversion of the chord.
- When the root of the chord is in the treble, and the first inversion chord is used, this creates a harmonic interval of a sixth. Intervals of thirds and sixths in harmony are very strong.

Second Inversion Chords

A second inversion chord is formed when the fifth note of the chord is placed on the bass. The chord of I used on the second inversion is written as Ic (c representing the second inversion). The only chord that should be used in the second inversion is the chord of I.

- The chord Ic is only to be used at a cadence point.
- The chord Ic is always followed by the chord of V or V7, then I or vi.

	Major Key	Minor Key
Perfect	Ic–V–I	ic–V–i
Interrupted	Ic–V–vi	Ic–V–VI

Question 5

Composing Bass Notes and Chord Indications to a Given Tune

Question 5 is a popular choice in the harmony section of the exam. Approximately 36 marks out of 60 are allocated to strong and musical chord choices. The remaining marks are given to the bass line.

What is Required to Get a H1 Grade in Question 5?

A H1 in the harmony section of the exam requires you to score 54 marks or above out of 60.

- One mark is given for each correct chord used (there are usually 24 chord boxes to be filled in).
- The quality of the chord progressions used is usually worth a maximum of 24 marks.
- Excellent chord progressions are usually awarded 11–12 marks.
- 0.5 marks are awarded per correct bass note under each correct chord symbol.
- The quality of the written bass line is important, as this is awarded up to 12 marks.
- Students are expected to include a sense of musicality management, an awareness of style (following on from the given bass line) and technical knowledge.

Checklist for Question 5

- Fill out the chord box.
- Make sure to include all suffixes, such as 'm' for minor and/or any # or ♭signs on chord symbols.
- Go through the given tune and mark out all potential correct chords for each chord box.
- Stick to using chord symbols or Roman numerals. Do not mix and match.
- Analyse the melody and identify any notes in the bar that are not harmony notes (not part of the chord). It may help to lightly pencil out these notes.
- Work out a cadence point. Does the music follow a four-bar phrase structure? Are cadence points marked by a long note or a rest?
- Pencil in your last two chords; these must make a finished cadence.
- Be mindful of good chord progressions.
- Pencil in an outline of the bass notes. Make sure your bass notes are the same as what is implied by the chord symbol or Roman numerals, e.g. if there is a D in the box, there is a D note in the bass.
- Be mindful of the spacing of your bass notes.
- Analyse the style of the given bass and try to work this into your bass composition.

- Double-check that you have the correct amount of beats in each bar.
- Make sure to end on a long tonic note.
- If the question is in the minor key, check that you have raised the seventh note (if used) in the bass line.

Leaving Certificate Exam 2020, Question 5: Sample Answer

This is a suggested solution. There are a number of other correct chord choices that can be inserted. The following sample will demonstrate good chord choices and how to follow on with a musical bass line.

Q.5 Composing bass notes and chord indications to a given tune

PREPARATORY WORK
Plot the chords available in the key of E flat major, either in the chord bank grid or on the stave below.

E♭ major has three ♭s: B♭, E♭, A♭

Notes of Chord					A♭		A♭
	B♭	C	D	E♭	F	G	A♭
	G	A♭	B♭	C	D	E♭	F
	E♭	F	G	A♭	B♭	C	D
Chord Symbol	E♭	Fm	Gm	A♭	B♭7	Cm	D°
Roman Numeral	I	ii	iii	IV	V(7)	vi	vii°

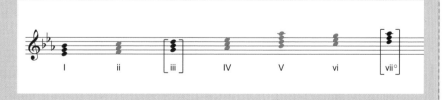

Step 1: Identify the chords

Fill in the chord box, remembering to include the dominant seventh.

Check for suffixes (m, ♭, b or c, etc.).

Notes of chord					A♭		
	B♭	C	D	E♭	F	G	A♭
	G	A♭	B♭	C	D	E♭	F
	E♭	F	G	A♭	B♭	C	D
Chord symbol	E♭	Fm	Gm	A♭	B♭7	Cm	D°
Roman numeral	I	ii	iii	IV	V(7)	vi	vii°

Step 2: Identify cadence points

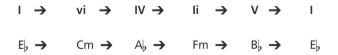

- A cadence is a **resting point** in the music and may be identified by a **long note** or a **rest** at the end of a phrase.
- Remember a cadence will give a **finished** or **unfinished** sound in the music.
- An unfinished cadence can be **any chord to the chord of V**, or the chords of V going to vi (the interrupted cadence).
- **The interrupted cadence** is commonly used in the second last phrase, so check to see if those chords will fit.
- There will be a finished cadence at the very end of the question; this may be V, V7–I or IV–I.
- **Avoid using inverted chords** at cadence points; the root chords give a stronger sound.

> **exam TIPS**
>
> Cadences are commonly (but not always) found at the end of each four-bar phrase.

Step 3: Chord progressions and filling in bass notes

Jot down **strong chord progressions** in E♭ major. An example of a strong chord progression in E♭ is:

I →	vi →	IV →	Ii →	V →	I
E♭ →	Cm →	A♭ →	Fm →	B♭ →	E♭

Look at the sample answer for bars 5 and 6*:

Please note that this is just a sample answer. There are a number of different ways to harmonise the melody.

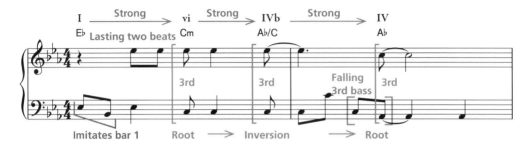

I–vi–IV is a strong chord progression.

In the third chord box above, chord IVb is strong as IVb sounds an interval of a third between bass and treble parts. Remember, third and sixth intervals are harmonically strong.

Bars 7–8:

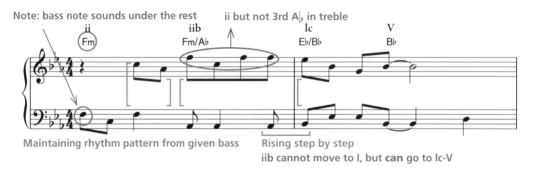

The bass note F is heard under the rest in the treble clef.

All of bar 7 appears to be the chord of ii. However, the first box in bar 8 appears to be the chord of I. The chord ii–I is not a strong progression, but iib or ii can go before the chord of Ic.

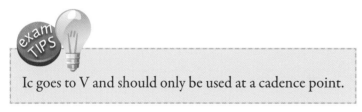

Ic goes to V and should only be used at a cadence point.

The rhythm and movement of the bass line imitates that of bars 1 and 2.

Bars 9–12:

There are only essential or harmony notes in the melody of bars 9–12.

The chord progressions used in bars 9–12 are **I–Ib–V–Vb–I–Ib–V–vi**.

The chord choices here are strong because of the intervals these chords create. Intervals of a sixth or a third are **strong harmonic intervals**.

The intervals are place between root position chords: **I–Ib–V–Vb–I–Ib–V–vi**.

The cadence in bar 12 (the penultimate phrase) is an interrupted cadence **V–vi**.

> The interrupted cadence V–vi is known as the 'surprise cadence'; we expect a finished sound (V–I) but hear a minor chord instead. Check the question to see if it would fit at the end of the penultimate phrase.
>
> Be mindful of where the chord boxes are placed in each bar. In the 2020 exam question, some of the chords fell on the offbeat.

Bars 13–16:

The chord choices in bars 13, 14 and 15 are tricky. Again, all of the notes here appear to be harmonic notes.

The use of the chords iib–ii gives a strong falling third in the bass line of bar 13. The use of ii–V gives a strong rising fourth in the bass line. These chord progressions, along with the continuation of the bass style, creates a musical harmony to the given melody.

A finished cadence is always required at the end of this question. Here, a plagal cadence (IV–I) in bar 16 fits with the melody.

The last note in the bass line is a long tonic note. This creates a strong and final ending.

Leaving Certificate Exam 2019, Question 5: Sample Answer

Q.5 Composing bass notes and chord indications to a given tune

PREPARATORY WORK
Plot the chords available in the key of C minor, either in the chord bank grid or on the stave below.

Notes of Chord	G E♭ C	A♭ F D	B G E♭	C A♭ F	F D B G	E♭ C A♭	F D B
Chord Symbol	Cm	D°	E♭+	Fm	G	A♭	B°
Roman Numeral	i	ii°	III+	iv	V(7)	VI	vii°

The notes that are crossed out are non-chordal or non-essential notes. Establish where these notes occur in the melody line. This should make it easier to establish which chords to use.

PN = passing note

AN = auxiliary note

Analysis of given bars 1–4:

The sample answer for this question is based on what happens in the opening bars.

PN = passing note

AN = auxiliary note

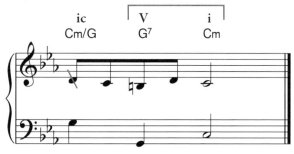

- The unessential notes (passing and auxiliary notes) have been marked out with blue.
- There is a raised sixth and a raised seventh in bar 4. These are highlighted to remind us to watch out for these notes when using the chord of V. (See section on melodic minor scale in Chapter 4: Melody.)
- The notes in the chord are marked out in red. This helps to keep a musical connection with the bass line in the rest of the bars.
- The bass line in the given bars consists of broken chords. There are no unessential notes.

Use of ic–V:

The transition ic–V should be only used at a cadence point. Look at the use of ic–V in the last bar of this sample answer:

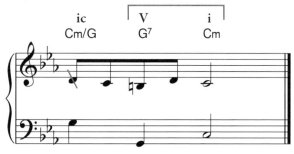

The first beat is treated as an **accented passing note**.

Alternatively, this ending could be written as follows:

Points to note:

- Over half of the marks for this question are awarded for your chord choices and input of bass notes.
- It is very important to analyse the given material and continue in that style.
- Make note of all possible chord possibilities and make your decision on strong chord progressions and harmony.
- Do not use the same chord in two consecutive chord boxes.
- Avoid using inversions for the sake of using them; they are weaker than root position chords and are used between root position chords.
- Check your note spacing and make sure your bass note corresponds to the chord name. You may lose marks if spacing is incorrect.

Question 4

Question 4 is another popular choice for the harmony question on the composition paper. The chords are given in this harmony question and students are required to compose melody and harmony to a given four bars of music. You may feel that the bass line is easier to complete in this question than in Question 5, as the chords are given. However, it is important to be aware that only **20 marks out of 40** are allocated to the bass line. The other 20 marks are awarded to the melody.

When preparing for Question 5 on the composition paper, take a look at Question 4 on recent past papers. Study the patterns in this question and note strong and common chord progressions.

How to achieve a H1 grade in Question 4

To achieve a H1 grade in this question:

Your bass line must:

- correspond with the chord that is in the chord box
- demonstrate an excellent awareness of style and shape.

Your melody line must:

- have a very high standard of style and imagination
- reflect a thorough awareness of key and underlying harmonic structure
- contain an excellent development of opening ideas
- demonstrate an excellent sense of directions and climax.

Leaving Certificate Examination 2020, Question 4: Sample Answer

Q.4 Composing melody and bass notes from a set of chords

PREPARATORY WORK
Plot the chords available in the key of E major, either in the chord bank grid or on the stave below.

Ab major has four ♭s: B♭, E♭, A♭, D♭

Notes of Chord	B G# E	C# A F#	D# B G#	E C# A	A F# D# B	G# E C#	A F# D#
Chord Symbol	E	F#m	G#m	A	B(7)	C#m	D#°
Roman Numeral	I	ii	iii	IV	V	vi	vii°

Analysis of given bars:
Bass line bars 1–4:

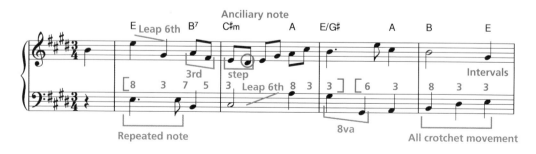

The rhythm is different between the treble and the bass on each beat of the bar.

There is less movement in the bass when there are quavers in the treble part.

Repeated notes, step movement and leaps are highlighted in the bass.

Treble line bars 1–4:

The melody line almost entirely consists of harmonic notes. There is only one non-essential note (auxiliary note) in bar 2.

Intervals between bass and melody are marked out. Thirds and sixths make strong harmonies.

Take note of the rhythm pattern of the melody line and the long note at the end of the phrase.

Points to note:

- The chord name corresponds with the bass note directly under the chord. You can then move off the note.
- There are the correct amount of beats in the bar.
- The line is clear and easy to read/play.
- The bass line musically connects and is developed out of the given bass line. This will demonstrate an excellent musical awareness.
- Mark out phrases and cadence points as you would do for Question 1 (there are no extra marks for this but it will give you a sense of structure).

- Try to get a sense of the given melody by singing it back in your head and/or marking in tonic solfa (whatever method you have practised in class).

> Mark in the intervals between the bass and the treble parts. If you notice a pattern of thirds and sixths, your harmony will be strong.

- Your melody must demonstrate an awareness of the key and the underlying harmonic structure. Use harmony notes as the basis of your melody.
- Keep a close eye on the intervals between the bass and the melody notes. Avoid too many consecutive octaves or intervals of a fifth.
- End on the tonic note.
- When composing in the minor key, be mindful of the rules that apply to the treatment of the sixth and seventh notes.

7 The Practical Exam

> **aims** By the end of this chapter, you will be able to:
> - understand the options available for the practical exam
> - be aware of the marks awarded and how to achieve optimum marks in the practical section
> - understand the criteria for music technology and the unprepared tests.

The majority of Leaving Certificate Music students opt to do the practical exam as their **elective** activity. This means that the practical is worth 50% (200 marks) of the available marks. 180 marks are allocated to performance and 20 marks are allocated to the unprepared test.

- The exam is usually held just before or just after the Easter holidays.
- Students are expected to demonstrate a standard of five years' classroom-based learning.
- The exam lasts 25 minutes for Higher Level elective, 20 minutes for Higher Level and 10 minutes for Ordinary Level.
- All candidates will take an unprepared test as part of the practical exam.

Resources for the Practical Exam

There are two documents that are important when preparing for the practical exam.

1. Notes for the Information of Teachers and Students

Coimisiún na Scrúduithe Stáit
State Examinations Commission

Leaving Certificate Examinations in Music, 2021
Practical Examinations

Notes for the Information of Teachers and Candidates

Please read carefully before filling out LMP4A forms.

This document is sent to schools each year between October and the Christmas break and can also be found at www.examinations.ie. The notes contain very important information about the exam. It is very important to read through the notes with your teacher as there may be some small changes or alterations made to the exam.

2. LMP4A Forms

| LMP4A | Leaving Certificate Music 2021
Higher Level Elective (One Activity) | HE1 |

Please read the *Information Note* carefully before filling out this form.

School No. _____   School Name: _____

Exam No: _____   Name: _____ D.O.B: _____

| Performing skill to be assessed (Tick one) | | Instrument/Voice: _____ |

Solo ➝ ☐ Solo singing   ☐ Solo playing   ☐ Solo singing to own   ☐ Conducting   ☐ Solo improvising
                                                        Accompaniment

Group ➝ ☐ Singing as a   ☐ Playing as a member   ☐ Improvising as a
              member of a group   of a group / Accompanying   member of a group

This form will be filled in prior to your exam and will be presented to the examiner on the day of your exam. There are a number of different LMP4A forms; complete the one that corresponds to your level and activity choices. You must fill in school details, your date of birth and exam number on the form.

There is a specific form for each different variation of the practical exam.

Form Name	Variation
OL	Ordinary Level
OLT	Ordinary Level Technology
HL	Higher Level
HE1	Higher Level elective, one activity
HE1T	Higher Level elective with Technology as activity
HE2	Higher Level elective, two activities
HE2T	Higher Level elective, two activities including Technology as one activity

Level	Requirements	Percentage
Higher Level	Three pieces in any one activity + Unprepared test	25%
Higher Level elective	Six pieces in any one activity + Unprepared test *or* Four pieces in two different activities + Unprepared test	50%

exam TIPS

You can choose your choice of activities and create your own programme. Explore the combinations of activities you can do and make your decision based on what you enjoy and work best at.

Performing Skills

There are a wide range of performing skills available for examination.

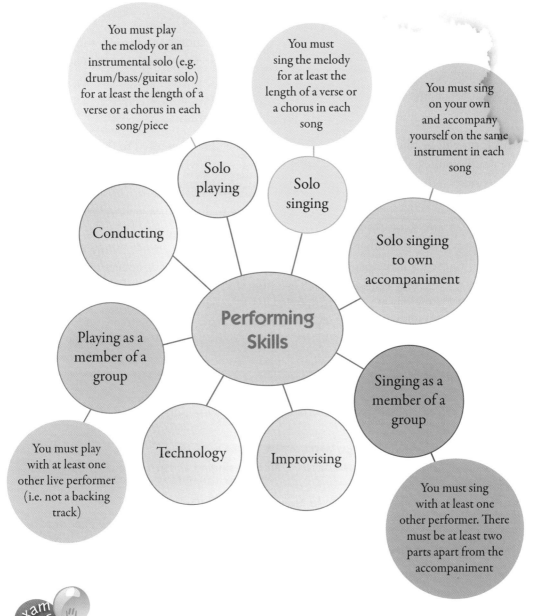

You must play the melody or an instrumental solo (e.g. drum/bass/guitar solo) for at least the length of a verse or a chorus in each song/piece

You must sing the melody for at least the length of a verse or a chorus in each song

You must sing on your own and accompany yourself on the same instrument in each song

Solo playing

Solo singing

Conducting

Solo singing to own accompaniment

Performing Skills

Playing as a member of a group

Singing as a member of a group

You must play with at least one other live performer (i.e. not a backing track)

Technology

Improvising

You must sing with at least one other performer. There must be at least two parts apart from the accompaniment

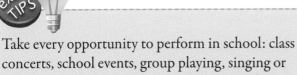

exam TIPS

Take every opportunity to perform in school: class concerts, school events, group playing, singing or instrumental groups, etc. The more you perform, the more prepared you will be for exam day.

Choosing Your Activity

Here is some important information from the 2020 student and teacher information notes. If you do not comply to the requirements, you may lose marks.

Solo Singing

- You must sing the melody for **at least** the length of a chorus or a verse in each song.
- There may not be another candidate singing the melody or harmony while you are singing your solo.
- An instrumental accompaniment (live or a backing track) may be added.
- Backing tracks may not be streamed live from the internet.
- The melody may not be doubled on a backing track.

Solo Playing

- You must play the melody or instrumental solo (e.g. drums, bass, guitar) for at least the length of a verse or a chorus in each song/piece.
- There may not be another performer singing or playing the melody during you solo.
- An instrumental accompaniment (live or a backing track) may be added.
- Backing tracks **may not be streamed live from the internet**. If you are playing the melody, the melody **must not be doubled** in the backing track.
- If you are not playing the melody, **there must be a solo section built into each piece** where the melody is not being played or sung on the backing track at the same time.

Solo Singing to Your Own Accompaniment (SSOA)

- You must sing on your own and must accompany yourself on the same instrument for each song.
- No one else (live or a backing track) can perform a with you.
- This performing skill is only to be chosen if both singing and accompaniment are to be assessed.
- If only the singing is to be assessed, then choose 'solo singing'.
- If only the accompaniment is to be assessed, then choose 'playing as a member of a group'.

Singing as a Member of a Group

- You must sing with at least one other live performer (i.e. not a backing track).
- There must be at least two other live parts apart from the accompaniment.*
- A backing track may be added to the performance, but the melody line must be performed live.
- Backing tracks may **not** be streamed live from the internet.
- There cannot be more than two voices/instruments per examinable part.

Playing as a Member of a Group

- You must play with at least one other live performer (i.e. not a backing track).
- There must be at least two other live parts apart from the accompaniment.*
- In the case of non-melodic instruments only (e.g. drums/bass guitar/rhythm guitar), a piano/keyboard/harp/guitar/ukulele player playing the melody with chords qualifies as one of the parts.
- A backing track may be added to the performance, but the melody line must be performed live.
- Backing tracks may not be streamed live from the internet.
- There cannot be more than two voices/instruments per examinable part.

* Accompaniment in this respect refers specifically to instruments that can supply backing of a chordal nature, i.e. piano, harp, keyboard, guitar or ukulele. Other accompanying instruments such as drums, percussion and bass guitar are considered as individual parts in a group performance.

Combinations

Many students choose to present more than one activity in the exam. It is very important that you are aware of combinations that you can and cannot do.

When considering two activities, note that the same instrument/voice may not be presented in two activities **unless one activity is solo and the other is a group**.

When presenting **solo singing to own accompaniment (SSOA)**, be aware of the following points:

- SSOA may **not** be combined with another SSOA
- SSOA may **not** be combined with solo singing
- SSOA may **not** be combined with group playing (unless you choose to play a different instrument)
- SSOA may be combined with group singing
- SSOA may be combined with solo playing

There are a selection of instruments that can be played within **one activity** but cannot be presented in **two activities** unless one activity is group and the other activity is solo. The instrument combinations that can be used within one activity are:

- Flute and piccolo
- Concert flute and traditional flute
- Tin whistle and low whistle
- Acoustic guitar and six-string electric guitar (not six-string bass guitar)
- Banjo and mandolin

- Piano and electronic keyboard
- Any combination of recorders
- Any combination of saxophones
- Any combination of percussion instruments

If you wish to present a combination of instruments that is not listed, you will have to apply in advance to the Practicals Section of the State Examinations Commission for written permission to do so.

Backing Tracks

You are not permitted to live stream a backing track during your exam. If you are using a backing track, make sure to download it and have a **hard copy** to play during your exam. It is best practice to have this prepared well in advance of exam day.

A hard copy can be in the form of:

- CD
- MP3 saved to a USB or a computer hard drive.

The use of mobile phones, computers or devices that are connected to the internet is prohibited.

Preparing for Your Practical

- Choose pieces that you will enjoy singing or playing.
- Incorporate regular practice time into your week.
- Try to have some variety in your programme, i.e. songs, pieces of different styles, different tempos, different keys, etc.
- Choose pieces that you will feel comfortable and relaxed performing: you are being examined on five years' classroom-based practical experience.

Music Technology

Music Technology is a popular choice of activity for both Higher Level and Ordinary Level students. A number of music software programmes can be used for this activity, including MuseScore, Sibelius, Finale Notepad and GarageBand.

Format of the Examination

A. First part of examination – input, edit, print/record, save and retrieve

All technology candidates will be asked by the examiner to:

1. Set up the score(s) to be input.
2. Input all or part of each part/track (the examiner decides). Music is input track by track.

3. Make the required number of edits.

- Edits must be performed on the score input on the day of the examination. Under no circumstances will candidates be permitted to perform edits on a pre-saved score.
- Candidates will be asked to play back the score after inputting and after each edit is executed.

4. Demonstrate how to record or print the score.

5. Save, close and retrieve the file.

B. Second part of examination – perform to own backing track*

(Higher Level one activity (H1T) and Higher Level elective one activity (HE1T) candidates only)

1. Candidates will be asked by the examiner to describe how they compiled the backing track. For example:
   - The process (computer, sequencer or live musicians recorded)
   - The number of tracks
   - Instruments or sounds chosen for each track and the reasons for those choices
   - Difficulties (if any) encountered, e.g. with balance

2. Play the backing track.

3. Perform to the backing track.

*Or perform the required number of pieces from the electronic repertoire (i.e. perform two (H1T) or four (HE1T) pieces on electronic keyboard using the full range of keyboard functions).

Criteria for Music Technology

Higher Level elective, one activity (HE1) criteria

This option is best suited to students who are competent at using technology, and are also required to perform with pre-prepared tracks.

- Two scores of three parts (at least 32 bars)
- Six edits
- Demonstrate how to print or record
- Save, close and retrieve
- Play four pieces from an electronic repertoire or compile or play to own previously compiled backing track*

*Backing track must consist of at least three parts/lines of at least 32 bars each. You must show evidence of/describe the compiling of the backing track. The music input of part one of the examination may not be used for the performance element. The performance to your own backing track must be a solo performance.

Higher Level elective, two activities including Technology as one activity (HE2T) Criteria

- One score of four parts or two scores of two parts (at least 16 bars)
- Three edits
- Show how to print or record
- Save, close and retrieve

Higher Level criteria

- One score or two parts
- Three edits
- Show how to print or record
- Save, close and retrieve

Choice of Score

Many students choose to input a score that has four parts, e.g. a string quartet or a SATB choir.

You may choose to input two separate pieces that have two parts each.

Make sure your chosen piece has some variety in note values, i.e. a mixture of crotchets, quavers, minims, etc.

Give yourself plenty of time to practice inputting your chosen score(s) – you will feel more confident in the exam.

During the exam, take your time and check that your note inputting is correct bar-by-bar as you go along. This is a performance exam, and you want your final playback to sound correct.

SAMPLE SCORE FOR HE2T

String Quartet in A Minor by V. Conway

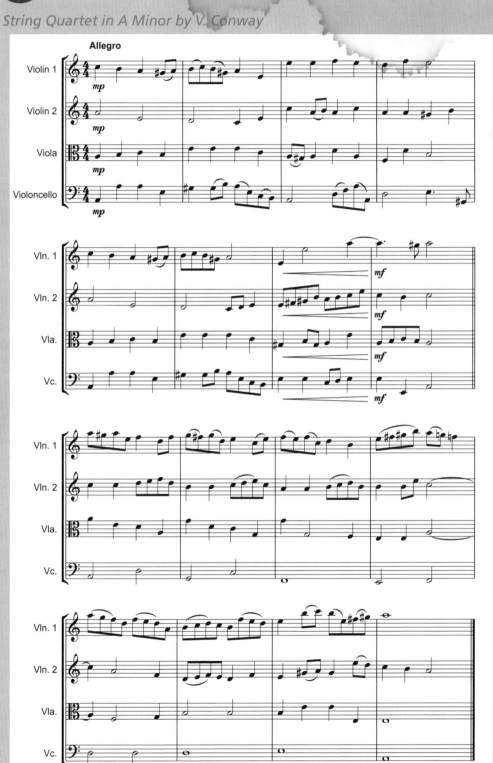

Edits

When making edits to your score, it is important to:

- make audible edits – the examiner can't mark what they can't hear
- choose edits that will make musical sense.

Some popular choices of edits are:

- changing tempo
- transposing the score
- changing dynamics
- adding/editing articulation
- changing note values.

Unprepared Tests

There are a wide range of unprepared tests that you can choose from. This part of the exam is worth 20 marks (twice the marks given to the Irish Music essay question). If you are taking the Higher Level elective, this means that this part of the music exam is worth 5% overall.

The choices of unprepared tests available to you include:

Test	Description
Aural Memory Melody (AMM)	Eight-bar melody played twice, student sings back; melody played a third time and student sings again. The student is marked on their best attempt.
Aural Memory Rhythm (AMR)	Eight-bar melody played twice, students claps back; melody played a third time and student claps back again. The student is marked on their best attempt.
Sight Reading Rhythm (SRR)	Student is given a minute to look over eight bars of rhythm. Student claps back rhythm. One attempt given.
Sight Reading Rhythm Guitar/ Ukulele	Student is given a minute to look over eight bars of chord sight reading. Student plays back chords. One attempt given.
Variety of Sight Reading Tests	Students can choose to sight read eight bars of music for a voice/ instrument/register of their choice. One minute given to look over the music. One attempt given.
Improvisation	Ordinary Level students are required to improvise eight bars of music. Higher Level students are required to improvise 16 bars of music.

Leaving Certificate Examination 2019, Unprepared Tests

Sight Reading Rhythm

Moderato

Moderato

Sight Reading Guitar

Moderato

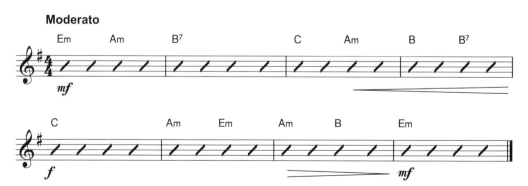

Sight Reading Ukulele

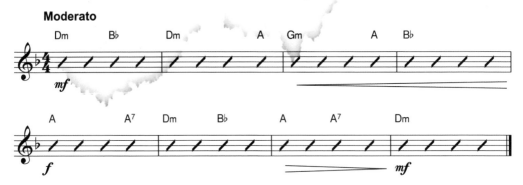

When approaching the unprepared test:

- Take your time to read through the music.
- 'Air' clap or play through the music. Do not clap/play out loud when reading through the test.
- Do not tap your foot or keep a pulse in the unprepared test.
- If you are doing the instrumental sight reading, watch out for tempo and dynamic markings.
- Try to keep a consistent flow and don't get put off by small errors; just keep going. You will lose more marks if you stop.